STOCK OPTIONS—

Getting Your Share of the Action

Also available from
BLOOMBERG PRESS

The Angel Investor's Handbook:
How to Profit from Early Stage Investing
by Gerald A. Benjamin and Joel Margulis
(July 2001)

Investing in Small-Cap Stocks: Revised Edition
by Christopher Graja and Elizabeth Ungar, Ph.D.

Zero Gravity Version 2.0: Launching Technology Companies
in a Tougher Venture Capital World
by Steve Harmon
(June 2001)

Investing in IPOs Version 2.0:
Revised and Updated Edition
by Tom Taulli

A complete list of our titles is available at
www.bloomberg.com/books

STOCK OPTIONS—

Getting Your Share of the Action

———◾———

Negotiating Shares and Terms in
Incentive and Nonqualified Plans

TOM TAULLI

Foreword by
BRUCE BRUMBERG

BLOOMBERG PRESS
PRINCETON

First edition published 2001
1 3 5 7 9 10 8 6 4 2

Library of Congress Cataloging-in-Publication Data

Taulli, Tom, 1968–
    Stock options—getting your share of the action : negotiating shares and terms
    in incentive and nonqualified plans / Tom Taulli.
        p. cm.
    Includes index.
    ISBN 1-57660-045-9 (alk. paper)
        1. Employee stock options. I. Title.

    HD4928.S74 T38 2001
    331.2'164—dc21

                                                                        00-069793

Edited by RHONA FERLING

Book Design by LAURIE LOHNE / DESIGN IT COMMUNICATIONS

To the love of my life,
my wife, Shauna

Contents

S e c t i o n   O n e

The Basics of Stock Options

S e c t i o n   T w o

Savvy Negotiations

Section Three

Living with Stock Options

Appendices

Acknowledgments

I OWE A GREAT DEBT of gratitude to the many individuals who have helped me write this book. They include: Gordon Peery, attorney with Stradling, Yocca, Carlson & Rauth; Walter Cruttenden and Frank Cutler, cofounders of E*Offering; Frank Marino, CEO of NetCapVentures; Chris Harano, CFO of Day Interactive; John Dunning, partner at Crossfire Ventures; Mark Prynn, director of business development at Deloitte & Touche; Tim Bei, director of business development at Internet.com; Jim Cravotta, financial consultant with Merrill Lynch; Scott Harvey, vice president of sales at RightStart.com; Adam Epstein, CEO of Superous; Bob Rieth, consultant with McKinsey & Co.; Rick Shultz, CEO of OptionWealth; and Bruce Brumberg, CEO of myStockOptions.com. I also want to thank Bloomberg Press for its support, as well as my editor, Rhona Ferling, who provided tremendous patience and guidance.

But most importantly, I want to thank my wife, Shauna. Her love and understanding were incredible. Thanks!

F o r e w o r d

CONGRATULATIONS: You own stock options. You're now one of almost 12 million Americans who have them. You might have received the options when you were hired or as an annual incentive, or you may have been awarded options as a special bonus. You're better motivated now and hope to get rich—or at least richer.

Like many of the readers of this book, you are passionate about your career and company. The stock options add that extra compensation spark for you. Your 401(k) plan and IRA are important, too, yet access to that money seems so far off, and it is meant for different purposes. The stock options make you feel like a company owner, or at least they enable you to dream about a house expansion, a long-desired European vacation, or perhaps Ivy League tuition for your triplets.

But don't start spending your expected jackpot now. Stock options are complex, and your gains are far from assured. Although stock options have become the juice of the New Economy's workforce, they are tough for many people to handle without some guidance, because they are filled with legal, tax, financial planning, and lifestyle intricacies. You'll have many questions and concerns on the road to newfound wealth through your stock options.

That's why Tom Taulli wrote this book—to help you manage these issues and maximize your stock options, your net worth, and your job satisfaction. It's your manual to the proverbial "Currency of the New Economy."

This highly readable, example-filled guide reflects the realities of the way people think about stock options and how they fit them into their lives and employment goals. It's organized into three main parts: The Basics, Savvy Negotiations, and Living with Stock Options. This handy division of topics allows you to dive right in at your level of sophistication and satisfy your immediate information needs.

You will likewise enjoy reading this book from beginning to end. It colorfully presents the realities of the stock option world for those fixated on their stock options. Tom Taulli provides a practical blend of tax, legal, financial planning, and career information, including checklists and memorable real-world stories.

So if you're new to the options game, spend time reading The Basics, which contains chapters explaining how stock options work, the different types of options, and their tax and securities law treatment. Getting ready to look for a new job or negotiate a raise? Then the section on Savvy Negotiations deserves your close review. It contains chapters with advice and plentiful illustrations on evaluating your option grant terms, options in private companies, and even details on foreign-company option plans.

When the time approaches for you to exercise your options and enjoy "the good life" that I hope they bring, the last section, Living with Stock Options, contains chapters on finding good advisers and on wealth-building strategies. The book even covers the much-avoided but all-too-important topics of stock option issues in divorce and estate planning.

May your stock option riches and job satisfaction match the wealth of knowledge that you gain from this book!

BRUCE BRUMBERG
CEO and Editor-in-Chief, myStockOptions.com

STOCK OPTIONS—

Getting Your Share of the Action

I n t r o d u c t i o n

S TOCK OPTIONS HAVE BECOME the new currency of
employee compensation, and not just among the ranks of
top executives. In more and more companies, all employees are getting stock options, contracts that allow them to buy
stock at a fixed price, even if the market value of the stock rises.

Along with asking for a nice salary, health benefits, and a 401(k)
plan, many job candidates are now demanding stock options. And
there is even a trend within the trend: during the early years of the
Internet boom, employees would accept a low salary in exchange for
stock options; now they are starting to get high salaries as well as
stock option grants.

As prosperity creates tight labor markets, employers are using
stock options as a way to attract and retain qualified employees.
Employers like using stock options because they encourage people
to work for the good of the company; the employee, in a sense,
becomes an owner and partner.

Stock options are not just concentrated in the fast-paced Silicon

Valley companies, either. Many companies with more traditional products—such as Starbucks Coffee Company—use stock options to elicit high levels of productivity from their employees. In Wal-Mart stores, the company's worker-owners can find Wal-Mart's current stock price posted above this reminder: "Tomorrow's price depends on you."

The National Center for Employee Ownership (NCEO) conducted a comprehensive study of stock options between 1998 and 1999. The study covers ninety-six companies, ranging from start-ups to *Fortune* 500 companies. NCEO, a nonprofit organization with 2,700 members, is considered a leading source of information on employee ownership.

According to its study, workers at these companies receive from 12 percent to 20 percent of their annual compensation in the form of stock options. The average value of these options is estimated at $41,000 for technical employees, $37,000 for professional employees, and $12,500 for administrative employees. Most of the companies surveyed provided stock options to all of their full-time employees, and 41 percent of the companies offer part-time employees opportunities to get stock options.

Entrepreneur Bill Gross wrote an article about this for the *Harvard Business Review* (November/December 1998, page 67). He is the founder of the CD-ROM developer Knowledge Adventure as well as the Internet incubator Idealab! Since 1998, Idealab! has taken public such companies as CitySearch and GoTo.com.

In the article, Gross talks about a management concept called "the new math of ownership." He states, "The multiplicative effect of setting employees free and giving them significant equity has a net positive result." He typically sets aside 30 percent of the equity of the company for the management team and employees. The CEO gets the largest share, which is about 10 percent of the total equity of the company. The remaining 20 percent is split among senior management and employees.

Some people have made huge fortunes from stock options in a breathtakingly short period of time. In February 1998, Meg Whitman was hired as the CEO of eBay, a leader in online auctions. She had left a position as general manager of the preschool division of Hasbro. It was a smart move. In 1998, she exercised options on 7.14 million shares of eBay, which were worth more than $1 billion. That made her the first female high-tech CEO to become a billionaire.

But options are not guarantees. For options to have value, the underlying stock must increase in value. According to a *Forbes* article (May 17, 1999, pages 211 to 213), of the 1,423 high-tech and biotech companies that went public between 1993 and 1999, 495 are trading below their offering prices. In other words, many employees have stock options with no current value.

Keep in mind that many other companies have not gone public and may never do so. As a general rule, most small companies fail within their first few years. In these cases, not only are the options worthless, the stock may be, too.

Some of the failures have been spectacular. A good example is PointCast, a company that distributed a screen saver that allowed users to access news and commentary. The technology became known as "push." For several months it was supposed to be the Next Big Thing. Billionaire Rupert Murdoch offered to buy PointCast for $450 million in early 1997. But PointCast thought this was too low and wanted to wring greater riches from the IPO market.

PointCast hired David Dorman, the former CEO of Pacific Bell. He received a boatload of options, ultimately giving him 10 percent of the company. Dorman got a signing bonus of $1.4 million. His base salary was $250,000, plus a potential cash bonus of $1.8 million. The company gave him loans amounting to $2 million, which allowed him to buy stock in PointCast. But his real coup was this: he got stock options to purchase 1,666,667 shares of PointCast at an exercise price of only $6 per share. In other words, as soon as PointCast had a successful IPO or was bought out, Dorman would have a big payday.

Unfortunately, push technology eventually fizzled, and so did PointCast. Dorman left the company, and with it, his stock options. In 1999, the company was sold for a mere $7 million to Idealab!

This perfectly illustrates why some well-regarded people do not believe in employee stock options at all. One such person is Warren Buffett, the famed investor who became a billionaire the old-fashioned way—by building his investment company, Berkshire Hathaway, through the accumulation of stocks in solid companies that he holds onto for long periods. Here are some reasons options are not all things to all people, including Buffett:

➤ **Bear markets.** The 1990s have seen an unprecedented bull market, and the buoyancy of share prices has pushed up the value of many people's stock options. But if the stock market goes into a prolonged bear cycle, as it did during the 1930s and again in the 1970s, then stock options are definitely not a good deal.

➤ **Resentment.** While many employees are making large sums of money from stock options, the wealth is still concentrated within the top tiers of management. For example, according to *The Economist* (August 7, 1999, page 18), in 1998, the CEOs of the top 200 companies in the United States averaged $8.3 million in options compensation. This lopsidedness may create resentment within a company, not to mention within the ranks of shareholders, who must buy their public company stock at the full market price.

➤ **Dilution.** The more options a company grants to employees, the more the stock value is diluted. This means that existing shareholders' percentage of ownership declines over time.

Despite all this, companies still like granting stock options. Besides motivating workers, stock options are enticing to companies for other reasons, such as the following:

➤ **Conserves cash.** Granting stock options does not involve any cash outlay for companies. This is especially beneficial for small companies, which seldom have much money in the bank. Stock options may, in fact, result in cash infusions into the company: in order to benefit from their options, employees must exercise them—that is, they must pay for the shares—and that cash goes straight to the company.

➤ **Offers favorable tax treatment.** As long as the current market value of a company's stock remains below the exercise price of the options, the company need not record the transaction on its books. There was a proposal to the Financial Accounting Standards Board in 1993 to make such transactions hit a company's bottom line, but it did not pass. Therefore, these transactions need only be placed in the footnotes of a company's financial statements.

The best approach with stock options is to be realistic. The press glamorizes the success stories, the way the eleven o'clock news zooms in on the game-winning home run. The fact is that hitting a home run is a tough thing to do. And so options are not always the major component in a compensation package. In fact, there are important non-monetary factors to look at, too: the corporate culture, type of work, benefits, freedom to make your own decisions, possibility for advancement, and corporate training.

Stock options have become more pervasive, but they are still new, they can be complicated, and there are few resources on how to analyze them. Only a handful of companies provide their employees with useful training materials.

This book rectifies that situation. We will look at the structure of option plans, as well as how to maximize their value. We will show you how the rules of the stock option game apply to your particular situation. For example, is your company private? Or has it recently done an IPO? Such basic considerations make a big difference, and that's where we'll start—with the definitions and concepts you need in order to make smart choices.

The intricacies of stock options keep many people from taking full advantage of them. The consequences of not understanding options can be quite severe—for example, it can cost painful amounts of money in unnecessary taxes. This book will give you the tools to maximize the value of your options—to make sure you get your share of the action.

Section One

The Basics of
Stock Options

Chapter 1 *r One*

What Are Stocks?

B EFORE WE CAN DEFINE stock options, we must define what a stock is. A share of stock represents partial ownership in a company, based on a finite number of shares that the company has issued. So, for example, if your company has issued 1 million shares and you have 100,000 of them, you own 10 percent of the company. This is also referred to as owning equity.

A share of stock has a current market price, determined by a bid-auction system on a stock exchange. To get listed on a stock exchange, a company must meet certain minimum standards for the size of its assets, the amount of its sales, and so on. If a company does get listed, the exchange will monitor it. If the company falls below the minimum standards, then the exchange has the right to delist (remove) it. Such companies will, in most cases, be transferred to another exchange with lower minimum standards. Delisting may also occur when one company purchases another.

There are several stock exchanges on which a company's stock may be listed:

New York Stock Exchange (NYSE; www.nyse.com). Founded in 1792, this is the oldest stock exchange in the United States. The exchange has a physical trading floor, on which professional traders buy and sell stock. The NYSE has the most rigorous listing standards of any stock exchange in the United States.

American Stock Exchange (AMEX; www.amex.com). This market, too, has a physical trading floor and is based in New York, although the AMEX caters primarily to medium-size companies. The AMEX merged with Nasdaq in 1999.

National Association of Securities Dealers Automated Quotation System (Nasdaq; www.nasdaq.com). This market does not have an actual trading floor; it is purely an electronic exchange. Created in 1971, Nasdaq has grown quickly, routinely trading more than 1 billion shares on any given day. For the most part, smaller companies list on Nasdaq.

Regional exchanges. These are U.S.-based exchanges that cater to specific regions of the country. Examples include the Philadelphia Exchange (www.phlx.com) and the Pacific Stock Exchange (www.pacificex.com). These markets focus primarily on small companies in their regions.

Bulletin Board Exchange. This, too, is an electronic exchange. The companies are fairly small and the trading volume low. Many so-called penny stocks (shares trading below $1) trade on this exchange.

Foreign exchanges. Most developed countries have their own stock exchanges. Some of the larger foreign companies list their stocks not only on the exchange in their home market but also on a U.S. exchange, such as Nasdaq or NYSE.

A foreign company that is listed on a U.S. stock exchange is traded through an investment instrument called an American Depositary Receipt (ADR). Here's how it works: A foreign company will deposit some of its shares in a bank. A bank will then issue ADR shares against the deposit. The bank will handle the many administrative concerns, such as dividend payments, taxes, and currency conversion.

If a stock is not listed on an exchange, then it is a private company. In that case, it is very difficult to sell your shares or even to know what they are worth. If you can find a buyer, the price you will be offered typically will represent a steep discount from what you would get if you had access to lots of buyers.

Life Cycle

IF A COMPANY GROWS and makes profits, its shares should rise in price. Of course, entire markets sometimes fall—because of national or world economic events—in which case even profitable companies may plunge.

A company may decide to reinvest its profits, plowing them back into operations, especially if it has ample growth opportunities. A company may also pay part or all of its profits to its shareholders in the form of cash dividends (this is usually the case with mature companies, such as utilities).

The rewards of owning stock can be huge. Investing in such companies as Microsoft and Cisco has made many people multimillionaires. But keep in mind that stocks are risky. For example, in the event of a bankruptcy, it is the shareholders who are last in line to collect any remaining assets of the company (first dibs go to the creditors, such as the IRS, bondholders, and other lenders). And although it seems obvious, remember that stocks go down as well as up.

Types of Stock

SOME COMPANIES ISSUE more than one class of common stock. A typical nomenclature for this would be Class A and Class B stock. The former usually gives the shareholder more voting rights at the company's annual meeting. Some classes of stock are made up of nonvoting shares.

There is also preferred stock. This type of equity is usually issued to major investors in a company, who are looking for extra protection. For example, in the event of a liquidation, preferred stockholders will get repayment before common stockholders. As a rule, preferred shares carry fixed dividend payments. In most cases, stock options apply only to common stock, not to preferred stock.

A company might issue warrants for sale to investors or as part of a stock issue. A warrant allows an investor to purchase a certain amount of stock for a fixed price during a certain period of time. For example, XYZ issues a warrant to Joe. The warrant covers 10,000 shares and has an exercise price of $10 per share, and it can be exercised within the next ten years. If the value of the stock is $20, then the warrants are worth $100,000 (10,000 shares times $10 per share in value above the exercise price).

A warrant is very similar to a stock option, but there are differences. The most important is that stock options are compensation for services performed, while warrants are for investors in a company or for key business partners. Moreover, warrants do not have vesting periods; that is, you can exercise your warrant at any time until the expiration date.

Stock Quotes

YOU CAN TRACK THE VALUE of stocks in the newspaper. If you prefer using the Web, you can find stock quote information readily at financial sites such as Motley Fool (www.fool.com), PCQuote (www. pcquote.com), and Bloomberg (www.bloomberg.com).

On the New York Stock Exchange, stocks are traded five days a week, from 9:30 A.M. to 4 P.M. The Nasdaq trades five days a week as well. However, it has after-hours trading, in which investors can buy and sell shares from 4 P.M. to 6:30 P.M. This is done with advanced electronic trading systems, called ECNs, or electronic communications networks. Some brokerage firms, such as E*TRADE and Schwab, offer clients after-hours trading (these firms have relationships with ECNs).

Here's an example of a stock quote for Yahoo!:

HIGH	LOW	STOCK	SYMBOL	VOLUME*	DIVIDENDS
250.17	28	Yahoo!	YHOO	22,431	$0.00

DIVIDEND YIELD	P/E	TODAY'S HIGH	TODAY'S LOW	CLOSE	CHANGE
0%	62	28⅜	25½	27¹⁵⁄₁₆	-0.22%

*$ thousands

The fifty-two-week high and low columns at the left show that during the past year, the stock has traded between $28 and $250.17 per share. Each stock has a unique identification, known as its ticker symbol. This term is a holdover from the days of ticker machines, which would ratchet out a long, thin strip of paper with the latest stock quotes. Yahoo!'s ticker symbol is YHOO.

The volume column shows how many shares were bought and sold during one day. The volume is usually expressed in thousands. Yahoo! traded about 22.4 million shares.

Volume is very important. If it is light—say 10,000 shares per day for a major NYSE stock—then there is probably not much interest in the company. As a result, the stock's price may stagnate. Such a thinly traded stock does not have much liquidity, either; that is, when you decide to sell your shares, you may find it difficult to get a good price.

You may have noticed that in our example, Yahoo!'s stock does not carry a dividend payment. However, if it did, a company would put this in the dividends column as a dollar amount per share, to be paid every quarter to shareholders. The percentage column computes the dividend yield of the stock. If Yahoo! had a 50¢ dividend, this would amount to $2 per year, or a 7.1 percent dividend yield ($2 divided by $27^{15}/_{16}$).

P/E stands for price/earnings ratio. Suppose a company has profits of $1 million annually, and it has 1 million shares outstanding (that is, shares owned by investors). This means it earned $1 per share ($1 million divided by 1 million shares). Now, suppose the company's stock is selling for $25 per share. Then the P/E ratio would be 25, which is $25 divided by $1 per share in earnings.

A P/E ratio is useful for computing the relative stock value of companies within a given industry. Suppose that while Yahoo! has a P/E ratio of 62, its competitors have P/E ratios of 20 to 40. This may indicate that Yahoo! is overvalued. It may also indicate that Yahoo! is a superior company, or at least that investors think it is. After all, Microsoft has historically had a high P/E ratio, but it is also a very profitable company, and investors will pay a P/E premium in order to own it. Finally, the quote shows the high and low for the trading day, and, at the far right, how much the stock went up or down from the previous day's close.

Market Indices

A MARKET INDEX QUANTIFIES and measures the general direction of prices of stocks or other securities. Most indices are totals expressed in terms of points. For example, you will see something like "The market rose 150 points today, to 1,150." Thus, in this case, the market opened at 1,000 and increased by 15 percent, which is 150 divided by 1,000.

There are many market indices, but the most common are the following:

Dow Jones Industrial Average (DJIA). This index covers thirty leading U.S. stocks, including such blue chips as IBM and Disney.

The DJIA is the most frequently quoted stock index.

Standard and Poor's 500 (S&P 500). As the name implies, this covers 500 companies. These are major companies with large market values. The breakdown is 400 industrials, 40 utilities, 20 transportation companies, and 40 financial firms.

Nasdaq Composite. This index includes all the stocks traded on the Nasdaq market. However, the index is heavily weighted by a small number of stocks, such as Microsoft, Intel, and Dell.

Russell 2000. This includes 2,000 small-capitalization stocks, meaning companies with less than $1 billion in stock outstanding.

Wilshire 5000 Index. This is a very broad index, including stocks from the New York Stock Exchange, Nasdaq, and the American Stock Exchange.

Earnings

THE VALUE OF A STOCK is determined primarily by how much profit a company will generate over its life. Of course, the more money a company makes, the more desirable the stock, all things being equal.

Every quarter, a company will report its earnings, meaning its profits after paying all expenses but before paying dividends. Often, Wall Street analysts make forecasts on these earnings. If a company does not meet these forecasts, there is typically a big sell-off of the stock. If the company exceeds expectations, the stock could soar.

Initial Public Offerings (IPOs)

AN IPO IS THE PROCESS by which a company sells shares to the general public for the first time. Wall Street investment firms, known as underwriters, facilitate the IPO. Examples of top underwriters include Goldman Sachs and Morgan Stanley.

Here's an example of how it works: XYZ Co. retains Goldman Sachs to do an IPO. Goldman Sachs performs due diligence on the company, a process of checking the books to make sure the company is in good enough financial shape to sell shares to the public. Goldman Sachs determines the number of shares to be offered to the public. In the case of XYZ, let's say the number is 5 million. A price is set at $10 per share. However, a company will not get the full $50 million (5 million shares times $10 per share). Rather, an underwriter will retain a certain percentage for its services. The industry standard is 7 percent. Once a company is public, its shares will then start trading every business day on a stock exchange.

Transacting Stocks

BUYING AND SELLING STOCK is done through a stockbroker. For employee stock options, your company may have a broker through whom you will deal (at least with the initial exercise of your options).

The most common type of order individuals place through brokers is the market order. This means that the broker is to buy or sell stock immediately, although even in the electronic age, "immediately" may take a few minutes.

If the stock is very volatile, you run the risk of its price changing before the trade is executed. A way to better control the price is to place a limit order. This specifies either the minimum price you will accept when an order to sell is made or the maximum price you will accept when an order to buy is made.

You should also be aware that there are two types of brokers.

Full-service brokers. These brokers provide personalized investment advisory services. For example, the broker will typically give advice on when to exercise your stock options or sell the stock and other investment strategies. Some brokers may also have a deep understanding of the stock option tax laws. Examples of full-service firms include Paine Webber, Merrill Lynch, Prudential Securities, and Morgan Stanley Dean Witter.

Of course, you must pay a commission for the service. In most cases, this is expressed as a percentage of the amount of the transaction. The fees can vary widely from firm to firm. Sometimes the commission can be several thousand dollars (if the transactions are, say, over $1 million). Moreover, there may be an account maintenance fee, which can run about $50 to $100 per year. Many brokers will negotiate their fee structures. It is worth a try.

Discount brokers. As the name implies, a discount broker provides transaction services at a lower rate than full-service brokers. Some discount brokers will charge less than $8 per trade, as long as you use the

Internet. Examples of such deep-discount firms include Datek and SureTrade. You will not get much in the way of personalized services; a discount broker assumes you have done your own homework. That said, more and more discount brokers are starting to offer a range of comprehensive services, including E°TRADE, Schwab, Ameritrade, Waterhouse Securities, and Discover Brokerage.

When opening a brokerage account, you have at least three types from which to choose.

Cash account. This is the most basic setup. Basically, you fill out a form on your background (bank reference, Social Security number, marital status) and risk tolerance, which refers to the types of investments with which you are comfortable. Then you write a check to deposit cash in the account (there are usually minimum amounts). Now you are ready to start transacting. When you buy stock, you must pay the seller within three business days (known as three-day settlement, or T+3).

Margin account. This is a more complex arrangement giving you the ability to borrow against the assets in your account. For example, suppose you have $10,000 worth of stock in your account. Your broker may allow you to borrow $5,000 against the account to purchase more stock or even to make personal purchases. For this privilege, you must pay interest to the broker. If the value of the account falls below a certain minimum amount, the brokerage firm has the right to require you to put either additional cash or stock into the account. If you don't, or can't, the broker will liquidate shares. This unhappy event is known as a margin call. You might be required to open a margin account when handling your stock options if you are doing cashless exercises (which will be explained in Chapter 4).

Cash management account (CMA). This is an account that sweeps all interest and dividends from your investments into a money market account, often on a daily basis. A money market account is a low-risk mutual fund that pays interest.

CMA accounts typically offer credit cards and check-writing privileges. The fees range from $50 to $100 per year, and the minimum amount required is about $20,000. Usually a CMA has a margin account built in, which you can choose to activate or not use at all.

Wrap account. These are special accounts that consolidate most of your assets in one place. A money manager is appointed to help select investments on your behalf. For this service, you pay an annual fee, expressed as a percentage of the assets in the account (usually 1.5 to 2.5 percent). Typically the minimum is $100,000.

With any brokerage account, you will get periodic financial statements detailing your holdings, transactions, gains, and losses. If your account is inactive, then you get statements only once every three months. When you buy or sell a stock, your brokerage will send you a confirmation, which documents the details of the trade (price, number of shares, date executed, and commission). These records are helpful for tax planning.

The shares you own are represented by a certificate, which specifies the number of shares. The back of the certificate contains signature lines that allow you to transfer the stock to a new owner. As a holder of common stock, you can either have the shares in your name or your stockbroker's name, which is known as "street name." This means that your broker will actually have physical possession of the certificates, holding them on your behalf. Actually, this makes it much easier to sell the shares, since the broker handles all the recordkeeping. Also, if the stock certificates are lost for any reason, the broker must rectify the problem, not you.

If you have a margin account, the certificates must be in street name, because the securities are being used as collateral for the loan. If you no longer want to use the services of a brokerage firm, you can have your account transferred. You are required to fill out some forms and might have to pay a small fee. It can take several weeks to complete the transfer.

Guarantees

IF YOU MAKE A BAD INVESTMENT, then you suffer the consequences. However, what if your brokerage firm goes bankrupt? What happens to your holdings then?

In the early 1970s, Congress set up the Securities Investor Protection Corporation (SIPC). This is an insurance fund that covers brokerage accounts of up to $500,000, of which $100,000 may be in cash. For a fee, some brokerage firms provide extra insurance coverage, such as $10 million.

Web Resources for Researching a Stock

NOT TOO LONG AGO, finding and assembling solid information about a company was not easy—or cheap. But with the advent of the Internet, this has changed radically. In fact, there is often *too much* information available for free; the trick is to find the most efficient ways to select what you want.

Here are some top resources:

Bloomberg (www.bloomberg.com). At this Web site, you have access to a plethora of financial information, including news; investment columns and commentary; technology stock analysis; and reports on initial public offerings, U.S. Treasuries, currencies, and mutual funds. Moreover, the site has great coverage of international markets.

CBS MarketWatch (www.cbsmarketwatch.com). This is a joint venture between Data Broadcasting Corp. and CBS. The site has been in existence since 1998 and is a leading source of financial news on the Web, featuring news stories and commentary from top analysts. The site also features a personal finance section, a "sector snapshot," and e-mail newsletters.

CNBC (www.cnbc.com). Until late 1999, CNBC's site was lacking on several fronts. Now it has a wealth of content that investors will find useful in getting news on specific companies. Important interviews and newscasts are archived on the site, and it also offers pages that focus on women's investment issues, loans, and tax topics.

Money (www.money.com). This site, produced by *Money* magazine, offers market coverage, online portfolio analysis, and tools for planning your retirement, finding the best mutual fund, calculating your returns, and more. It also features columnists writing about investing topics.

Money.com has a section devoted to employee stock options. Articles walk you through the basics, and the site also features a glossary, as well as an online calculator for stock options. Basically, the calculator shows the consequences of three sell strategies: (a) exercise your options, then hold the stock for a sale at a later date; (b) hold your options and exercise them later; and (c) exercise your options and immediately sell the stock. We'll explain all these strategies in Chapter 4.

Motley Fool (www.fool.com). As the name implies, the Motley Fool takes a playful approach to explaining investing, but its content is solid. Every day, the site features in-depth profiles of companies, as well as articles about taxes, investing basics, and retirement. Some of these financial planning articles cover stock options.

MSN Investor (www.investor.msn.com). MSN Investor has many of the same features as Yahoo! Finance. It has a tax section, which occasionally has stories about stock option planning. It also allows you to open a brokerage account and trade online.

Wall Street Journal Interactive (www.wsj.com). This super site is the bible for understanding what's happening in the business world. True, there is a subscription fee, but it is only $4.95 per month, and it is an incredible value. The *Wall Street Journal* has a great staff of writers, and its coverage is also comprehensive. More and more, WSJ.com has been covering stock option planning.

When you subscribe to *Wall Street Journal* Interactive, you also get access to *Barron's* Online. Another publication in the *Wall Street Journal* empire is *SmartMoney* (www.smartmoney.com), which is free online. The site is an excellent source for broad financial planning topics. The tax guide section has a variety of articles on stock options.

Yahoo! Finance (www.finance.yahoo.com). This is a simple site that organizes company information very well. When researching a stock, you can find all the necessary information here, including SEC filings, charts, analyst research, and news stories. The site also features a world-finance section that focuses on business developments in individual countries.

Yahoo! is particularly effective at personalizing financial information, in "My Yahoo! Finance." With this tool, you can track the latest news on your stocks, using parameters and templates that you set up and customize yourself.

Chat Sites

THE EMERGENCE OF THE INTERNET has introduced a new forum for investment: chat rooms. Basically, anyone can sign up and make his or her investment views known to the world. Some of the most popular investment chat rooms are found on the following sites:

➤ Motley Fool (www.fool.com)
➤ Ragingbull.com (www.ragingbull.com)
➤ Silicon Investor (www.techstocks.com)
➤ Yahoo! Finance (www.finance.yahoo.com)
➤ MSN Web Communities (www.investor.msn.com)

Take chat information with a grain of salt. On occasion you'll witness "flame wars," in which chat participants who disagree with other participants' views start calling one another names. Also, it is difficult—if not impossible—to know the identity of the participant and whether he is biased in some way. For example, a participant may be affiliated with the company he is promoting, or he may be a competitor. Or the person may have no ulterior motives but not know what he is talking about.

For all of these reasons, chat rooms can be a waste of time. Much of the information is of little value except as entertainment. And acting on it can be particularly harmful in the area of stock options, which are complex and require professional advice. It is usually better to rely on information that has gone through a filter, such as the articles on Motley Fool and the other Web sites mentioned above.

Chapter Two

What Are Stock Options?

A STOCK OPTION IS A CONTRACT between you and a company. The option gives you the right to buy a fixed number of shares in the company for a fixed price, called the exercise price. You have a limited time to purchase the shares, typically up to ten years. When a company grants you stock options, it must provide you with the following information:

Option contract. This contract sets out the terms between you and the company, such as:

➤ number of shares

➤ vesting

➤ exercise price

➤ type of option (nonqualified stock option or incentive stock option)

➤ termination (what happens in the event of death, disability, leave of absence, or discharge)

Option plan. This sets forth the general policies regarding a company's stock option plan. It will cover such things as:

➤ maximum number of shares available for grants

➤ eligibility for the options

➤ vesting

➤ changes in capital structure (that is, what happens if the company is sold or goes public)

A company may provide employees with other helpful information, such as answers to Frequently Asked Questions (FAQs), which anticipate the most common things employees want to know about their stock options; videos; seminars; and one-on-one meetings with benefits counselors or personnel from the company's human resources department. Increasingly, companies are posting stock option information on their corporate "intranets." But some companies do not yet provide good sources of extra information, which may be why you are reading this book.

When you are granted stock options, make sure you ask the person who administers the plan as many questions as you can. But keep in mind that this person is not allowed to provide personalized advice on matters such as your tax situation and when you should exercise your stock options. Those are examples of advice you should seek from a CPA, lawyer, or financial planner, as we'll see in Chapter 11.

And do not pay attention to what other employees are saying about the stock option plan. The grapevine spreads many plausible-sounding rumors, and buying into such scuttlebutt can lead to bad decisions about your stock options.

Note: A stock option that a company grants to an employee is not the same as options that are traded on the Chicago Board of Trade. Employee options, which are generally nontransferable, cannot be traded to the public.

Basics

LET'S TAKE AN EXAMPLE of a stock option. Suppose you work for Yahoo! and get stock options. They grant you the right to buy up to 3,000 shares over a period of three years for $50 per share. This is known as the exercise price. Usually when a company grants you options, the exercise price is the same as the current market price (on the day of the grant). So in our Yahoo! example, the company arrived at a $50 exercise price by using its current stock price of $50.

Options do not have any value unless the stock price rises above the exercise price. So if the stock price soars to $75, the value of your options will be $75,000. This is calculated by first subtracting the exercise price ($50) from the current price ($75) and then multiplying this difference by the number of shares (3,000).

Alas, there are restrictions on when you can actually take advantage of this potential wealth. The biggest restriction is the process known as vesting. Typically a company will have vesting periods that range from three to five years, meaning that you have to wait that long after the options are granted before you can exercise them. So let's say Yahoo! has a three-year vesting period and that after one year of working, you can exercise 1,000 shares; after two years, another 1,000 shares; and after three years, the remaining 1,000 shares. This is known as gradual vesting of your options on 3,000 shares. Some companies have "cliff vesting," in which all the options vest on a certain date.

Why have a vesting period before the employee can exercise the options? From a company's standpoint, it is a way to retain employees. If the employee leaves the company, any unvested options normally are voided, a fact that encourages employees to stay with the company and remain productive in return for potential future gains.

Now let's say the first year has gone by and Yahoo! stock is selling for $75 per share. You exercise the options—that is, you buy the 1,000 shares for $50 each (the exercise price). This costs you $50,000. You now own 1,000 shares of Yahoo! You can either hold on to the shares or sell them on the open market, a decision that has tax consequences, which will be discussed in Chapter 4. Some companies may mandate a holding period that prevents you from selling the stock immediately after you exercise the option, although this is rare.

On the other hand, suppose a year goes by and Yahoo! is selling for only $25. In this case, you would simply not exercise any options; it would be cheaper to buy the shares for $25 each on the open market than to pay $50 each by exercising your options.

Companies have widely varying policies on which employees get options. Some grant options to all employees, and even to part-time workers, as Starbucks does. Others grant options only to executives and key employees. Still others grant options based on performance measures.

Although a stock option gives an employee the right to buy stock, it does not represent ownership in a company. An option holder has no shareholder rights, such as rights to dividends, to vote, or to proceeds in the event of a liquidation. It is only when a stock option is exercised that an employee becomes a shareholder.

Fair Market Value

AT EVERY STAGE OF YOUR DEALINGS with stock options, it is critical to know the fair market value of the company's stock, which is tied directly to the real value of your options. The traditional definition of fair market value is "The price at which property would change hands between a willing buyer and a willing seller, both of whom are under no pressure to buy or sell and both of whom have reasonable knowledge of the pertinent facts."

When evaluating company stock, there are two types of fair market values:

Public values. These are the prices at which shares are being traded on a stock exchange. But even these public prices may be deceiving. For example, some stocks have very light trading volume, which is the number of shares traded on a daily basis. Top stocks—like Microsoft and Cisco—trade millions of shares every day. But smaller companies may trade only a few thousand shares per day. At most small or medium-sized companies, if you have vested options for 100,000 shares, you could encounter difficulty selling all of those shares on the open market without driving down the stock price.

Private stock. The share value of nonpublic companies is often difficult to estimate, because there is no freely trading market for the securities. One method of valuation is to look instead at recent sales of shares in that company. In that case, find out whether these stock sales were "at arm's length," which means making sure that there is not some conflict of interest between the buyer and seller (that is, the parties to the trade are brothers or belong to the same company).

Another approach is to hire an independent appraiser. Appraisers value the company on such things as asset values, profits, sales, or comparable valuations of other companies in the same industry. While the valuation could be subject to dispute in court (if, for instance, the appraiser was not a neutral third party), it is generally the best approach. Private companies that are backed by venture capitalists will typically use an appraiser.

Two Types of Taxes, Two Types of Options

THERE ARE TWO MAIN TYPES of options: incentive stock options (ISOs) and nonqualified stock options (nonquals). We'll discuss these in the next two chapters. For now, just know that many stock option strategies, and the decisions about which ones are best, revolve around taxes. To understand many of these approaches, you need to look at the differences between ordinary income taxes and capital gains taxes.

To encourage investment, Congress has been reducing the capital gains tax since the late 1980s. Currently short-term capital gains are taxed at the same rate as ordinary income, which can be as high as 39.5 percent. But if a capital asset—such as stock—is kept for at least one year, then the tax rate drops to 20 percent (this is known as a long-term capital gains rate). The idea behind this differential is to encourage long-term investing over short-term speculation.

There are three main components to the computation of your capital gains taxes. First of all, there is the cost basis. This is how much the IRS deems you invested in the capital asset when you acquired it. For example, suppose you buy 1,000 shares for $10 per share. Let's say you also pay your broker a commission of $100 to execute the trade. Your cost basis is the total cost of the transaction, or $10,100 (1,000 times $10, plus the $100 commission).

The second component of the calculation is the amount you receive when you sell the asset. Let's say you sell the 1,000 shares for $15 per share and pay another $100 commission. Your net proceeds from the transaction are $14,900, which is $15,000 ($15 times 1,000) minus $100 (the commission). This is known as the amount realized. To calculate the capital gain, you subtract the cost basis of $10,100 from the net proceeds of $14,900, for a capital gain of $4,800.

The third component of the calculation is the capital gains tax rate. This is only 20 percent if you held the assets for longer than one year but is otherwise the same rate you pay on ordinary income.

Of course, there are also capital losses, when your "capital gain" is a negative number. To alter the example, suppose you sold the stock for $5 per share and paid a $100 commission. This would bring you a total of $4,900 ($5 times 1,000, less the $100 commission). The capital loss would be $5,200. This number is calculated as $4,900 subtracted from the cost basis ($10,100).

When you file income taxes, you can deduct your capital losses against your capital gains. If you have more losses than gains, you can deduct up to $3,000 in net losses from your taxable income. Example: Suppose you have capital gains of $10,000 on one stock and $15,000 in capital losses on another stock. Your net loss is $5,000. You can deduct an extra $3,000 from your taxable income. You still have $2,000 in additional losses, which you can actually deduct in future tax years. This is known as a tax-loss carryforward.

When you have a capital gain or loss, your broker will send you a Form 1099-B. This shows the amount realized, positive or negative. You then put this information on a Schedule D for your tax return.

Ordinary income is compensation derived from providing services and is in the form of salary, bonuses, commissions, and in many cases, stock options. The maximum tax rate on ordinary income is 39.5 percent (this applies to income above $250,000). In fact, after factoring in the phaseout of deductions (such as the personal exemption) and state taxes, an individual's effective tax rate can exceed 50 percent. In other words, if your option income is treated as ordinary income, then not only is your tax rate higher, but you are subject to withholding for federal income taxes, Social Security taxes, and Medicare taxes. These taxes may sometimes be deferred. If you have bought or received restricted stock—stock that you are prohibited from selling and that is subject to a risk of forfeiture for a certain period of time— you do not owe taxes until the sale or forfeiture restrictions are lifted.

Because of these big differentials, people try to shift income toward capital gains. However, since employers typically get better corporate tax treatment for what they pay out as ordinary income, companies try to avoid having compensation treated as capital gains.

IRAs and Stock Options

UNFORTUNATELY, IT IS NOT LEGAL to put stock options themselves into an individual retirement account (IRA). An IRA is a special tax shelter geared for retirement. Each person can contribute up to $2,000 in earned income per year to an IRA. The gains on an investment growing within an IRA are not taxed until the money is withdrawn.

Furthermore, because IRA contributions must be cash, the stock that you receive upon exercise of an option may not be transferred to your IRA. You may not put any property into an IRA.

However, you can withdraw money from your IRA and then use the cash to exercise the options. You are allowed to withdraw money from your IRA for a sixty-day period without incurring a penalty or taxes.

Valuation Methods for Stock Options

ONE OF THE TRICKIEST ASPECTS of stock options is determining valuation. For example, suppose you work for a private company and are issued options to buy 10,000 shares. Since there is no public market for the shares, what is the real value of your options? Or let's say that you have options on 100,000 shares, but they do not vest for six months. In six months, the price of the underlying stock might shoot up by $10 a share, making you a millionaire, or the stock price might stay exactly what it was on the day the options were issued, making your options (so far) worth nothing.

Such valuation issues can be critical. For a company, if the estimate of valuation is too low, then more options would be issued, and the company's shareholders will suffer a higher dilution of their share value than they expected. Then again, if the company's estimate of valuation is unrealistically high, employees will receive fewer options. They may become disgruntled and perhaps even leave the firm.

There are three main valuation methods in use, and a company has the discretion to choose any of them, although the Black-Scholes method is clearly the standard. Let's take a look at it and at the other two systems.

The Black-Scholes method. The Nobel Prize–winning economists Fischer Black, Robert Merton, and Myron Scholes developed the Black-Scholes pricing model. To understand their method, you must take into consideration two concepts:

1   **Intrinsic value.** This basically means the degree to which the fair market value of the stock exceeds the option's exercise price. Let's say that a stock is selling for $20 and the exercise price of an option on that stock is $10. Then the option's intrinsic value is $10, and the option is referred to as being "in the money." If the stock

is selling at $10 or lower, the option has no intrinsic value. In this case, the option is "out of the money."

2   **Time value.** All options have a time value, even if at the moment they have no intrinsic value. For example, let's suppose in the case above that there is a possibility that the stock price could increase over the remaining time period of the option. So there is some possibility that you might be able to sell your stock option for $12, not $10. The extra $2 would be the time value. As an option gets closer to expiration, its time value tends to fall.

The actual Black-Scholes formula is extremely complex, involving the following elements:

➤ the strike price of the option
➤ the expiration date
➤ the future dividend yield (an assumption)
➤ the expected future volatility of the stock (another assumption)
➤ the risk-free rate (this is the rate of return on a very safe investment, such as a Treasury bill)
➤ the current stock price

Basically, the formula analyzes the time value and intrinsic value of an option. The calculation then provides a fair market value.

There have been many criticisms of this model. For example, how is it possible to make an accurate assumption about the future volatility of the stock, especially if the company has been private? In practice, future volatility is estimated by various techniques, such as looking at the volatility of comparable companies that are public. But criticisms notwithstanding, the model has been quite accurate, by and large.

If you want to do a Black-Scholes calculation, check out this Web site: www.numa.com/derivs/ref/calculat/option/calc-opa.htm. It has an online calculator, as well as sample calculations.

Moreover, you can find real-life Black-Scholes calculations in public company SEC filings, which are published at EDGAR Online (www.edgar-online.com). When you do your search, look for Form 10-K. Then find the section entitled "Accounting for Stock-Based Compensation." For example, Starbucks Coffee Company granted options in 1999, 1998, and 1997 that had valuations (based on Black-Scholes) of $8.86, $7.20, and $5.42 per share, respectively.

Present value of expected gain (PVEG). This valuation model attempts to guess the date at which the options will be exercised and the value of the options at that time. The variables for the calculation include:

➢ the current stock price
➢ the estimated growth rate (this is based on a stock index, like the Standard and Poor's 500)
➢ the risk-free interest rate (Treasury bill rate)
➢ the time until exercise (this is usually based on prior history of the company or industry)

Because the PVEG method is the only one that uses an estimated growth rate, it can be useful when options are based on achieving certain goals. For example, suppose the estimated growth rate for your company is 20 percent. If the company instead grows by 25 percent, then the option holders will see a bigger increase in the value of their options. The PVEG model takes that into account.

Face value method. This is by far the easiest calculation. It compares your stock options to those of another company. The big problem with this method arises when the comparison is made to a company that turns out not to be equivalent. In that case, the options can be severely undervalued or overvalued.

Examples of Company Plans

STOCK OPTION PLANS COME IN MANY shapes and sizes, and the plan often reflects the company's attitudes. The table below shows typical stock option grants for the technology industry. (See the table on the following page.)

As alluded to earlier, some organizations provide stock options only to upper management, whereas others grant options in some form to nearly every employee. Here are examples of two current employee stock option plans.

Starbucks Coffee Company
The CEO of Starbucks, Howard Schultz, is a firm believer in granting stock options as incentives for employees. In fact, he wrote about such policies in his autobiography, *Pour Your Heart Into It*. The cof-

Annual Stock Option Grant Practices in the High-Technology Industry

LEVEL	ANNUAL GRANTS AS A % OF SHARES OUTSTANDING	OPTIONS BASED ON 20 MILLION SHARES OUTSTANDING
CEO	0.3118%–0.4320%	62,360–86,390
Top Executive (2-5)	0.0853%–0.1728%	17,051–34,550
Director	0.0596%–0.1006%	11,914–20,120
Key exempt	0.0160%–0.0227%	3,195–4,547
Other exempt	0.0074%–0.0104%	1,484–2,072
Administrative	0.0049%–0.0074%	972–1,480

Source: Salary.com, based on data compiled from published surveys.

fee retailer was founded in 1971 in Seattle, opening its first store in Pike Place Market. In 1983, Schultz took a trip to Italy, where he saw many espresso bars (more than 1,500 in Milan alone). He thought he could create a similar coffee culture in the United States, but he had differences with the original founders and eventually started his own company. By 1985, Schultz was able to scrape together $3.8 million to buy Starbucks. There were still only eleven stores at the time.

In 1991, Schultz established an employee stock option plan. He knew that the coffee retail business was very competitive and had a high employee turnover rate. Stock options appeared to be a wonderful way to get a competitive edge in attracting and retaining qualified people.

Starbucks was the first major private company to offer a stock option plan to part-time employees as well as full-timers, along with other benefits, including health insurance, paid leave, and dental insurance. The move to stock options panned out. Now, of course, the company is a powerhouse, with more than 2,500 retail locations around the world. During 1999, the company generated $1.7 billion in revenues, up from $1.3 billion in 1998. Net earnings increased to $101.7 million from $68.4 million.

Suppose Starbucks hired you in 1995 and granted you options for 10,000 shares, with an exercise price of $5. The vesting period for all shares is four years. In early 1999, Starbucks had a 2-for-1 stock split. That is, for every share you owned, you got an extra one. This means you now have 20,000 stock options. What's more, the exercise price is cut in half to account for the fact that there are twice as many shares. In 1999, you decided to exercise your 20,000 shares and sell them at the current market price of $32.50. You would have had a gain of $600,000 (20,000 times $32.50 minus $2.50).

Ask Jeeves

Ask Jeeves is an innovative Web site on which users can pose any question in a natural-language format and receive several variants of that question to which the site has found answers. The goal of the company is to "humanize the Internet by making it easier and more intuitive for consumers to find information, products, and services." The company mascot, a graphical butler named Jeeves, serves up the findings.

In its first month of operation (April 1997), the site was getting 3,000 questions per day. By 1999, the site was getting more than 1 million hits per day. The IPO was in July 1999, and the stock was priced at $14. On its first day of trading, the stock surged to $65.

Three months before, in April 1999, the company's board had adopted a new equity incentive plan. It issued more than 2 million shares' worth of options, apportioned between incentive stock options for employees (Chapter 3) and nonqualified stock options for directors, consultants, and advisers of the company (Chapter 4). The plan is administered by the company's compensation committee, composed of three board members. This committee decides the option exercise price, which cannot be less than 100 percent of the fair market value of the common stock on the date of the option grant of the ISOs, and not less than 85 percent of the fair market value of the common stock for nonquals.

Options cannot be granted to any person who owns more than 10 percent of the total voting power of the company, unless the exercise price is 110 percent of the fair current market value of the stock. Plus, no more than 500,000 shares of common stock can be granted to anyone in any calendar year. The latter restriction is included to comply with Section 162(m) of the Internal Revenue Code, which has strict rules on the deductibility of compensation to certain executive employees when that compensation exceeds $1 million.

What Company Officers Received

LET'S SEE SOME EXAMPLES of what company officers received:

> **Robert Wrubel, CEO.** Before joining Ask Jeeves, he was the chief operating officer of Knowledge Adventure, an education software company. In his employment agreement, he got an initial base salary of $180,000. He was granted options of 675,000 shares with an exercise price of 46¢ per share. When he was promoted to CEO, he received an option grant for an additional 375,000 shares at an exercise price of 73¢ per share. Subsequently he got another grant of 200,000 shares, with an exercise price of $10. These options vest over a four-year period (the vesting period starts on the date of each grant).

> **Edward Briscoe, senior vice president and general manager, Consumer Question Answering Service.** Before joining Ask Jeeves, he was president of global sales at Iomega. He received a base salary of $170,000 and an option to purchase 400,000 shares at an exercise price of 73¢. The first 100,000 shares vested in January 2000, and 8,333 shares vest at the end of each month thereafter.

> **M. Bruce Nakao, chief financial officer.** The former CFO of Puma Technology came to Ask Jeeves with an initial base salary of $175,000. He received an option to purchase 250,000 shares at $9.50 per share.

> **Laurence G. Fishkin**, senior vice president of business development. Before hiring on at Ask Jeeves, he was the vice president of business development for Relevance Technologies. His compensation package included a salary of $130,000 and an initial bonus of $50,000. He got an option grant of 225,000 shares at an exercise price of 73¢ per share.

As you can see in the box at left, these option grants have varying strike prices—from 46¢ to $10 per share. There are several reasons for this. First, it is common for executives to get successive option grants over time—especially when they are promoted (this was the case with the CEO). Second, the value of the company's shares increased substantially over a short period, because the company was growing very fast, and the exercise price of the options being issued was adjusted in tandem with that rise in share value.

Conclusion

THIS CHAPTER BUILDS the necessary foundation to understand the basics of employee stock options. Note that even some top executives do not understand these basics. In the next two chapters, we will discuss in detail the two types of employee stock options: incentive stock options and nonqualified stock options.

Incentive Stock Options

INCENTIVE STOCK OPTIONS (or ISOs for short) are not as common as nonqualified stock options, which will be explained in the next chapter. ISOs have special tax features that can be particularly beneficial for the employee.

When you are granted an ISO, you do not owe any taxes. Even if the options vest and you do not exercise them, there is still no tax. This may seem self-evident, but as we shall see with nonqualified stock options, it is possible to owe income taxes when the options are granted.

Generally, you will owe taxes on ISOs when you either exercise the options or sell the stock after exercising the options. Depending on the circumstances, the taxes may be based on the alternative minimum tax (AMT), ordinary income, or capital gains. Before looking at these tax structures, let's first understand how a stock option grant is classified as an ISO.

Criteria for ISOs

HOW DO YOU KNOW IF THE OPTION you have is an ISO or a nonqualified stock option? Of course, your company will tell you, and it will also be stated in your option agreement, but here are the rules, for your reference:

➤ **Nontransferable.** An ISO is nontransferable. That is, you cannot gift an ISO except by death, in a will or trust. This is a tax law requirement.

> **Option plan.** An ISO must be granted in accordance with a company option plan, which sets forth the basic terms of the company's option policies. Furthermore, ISOs cannot be granted more than ten years after the plan has been established (that is, after ten years, a new plan must be drawn up). Interestingly enough, the principal requirements for a stock plan are minimal. The only specifics that must be in writing are the total shares to be granted and the types of employees eligible for the options. The company's board of directors must approve the option plan, and shareholders must approve it within twelve months of the directors' approval.

> **Length.** An employee may not exercise an ISO later than ten years after the option grant. If an option holder owns more than 10 percent of the company's voting stock, then the time frame is five years.

> **Exercise price.** The exercise price cannot be lower than the current fair market value of the stock at the time of the options grant. If the employee owns more than 10 percent of the voting stock, then the minimum exercise price is 110 percent of the current fair market value.

> **Employment.** ISOs can be issued only to people who are company employees at the date of the grant. If the employee leaves the company, he or she has three months to exercise the options.

> **Leased employees.** Professional employer organizations (PEOs) lease employees to client companies, but these leased employees are not eligible to receive ISOs from the client company.

Warning: On rare occasions, an employer may change your options from ISOs to nonqualified stock options. Of course, this would wipe out your tax advantages. The best way to prevent this from happening is to have your lawyer help you draft a clause to insert in your options contract preventing the company from making such a modification.

Now, depending on the policy of your employer, you may be eligible to receive both ISOs and nonquals. In fact, this may be necessary for the $100,000 rule.

Suppose your company grants you 100,000 options at a $10 exercise price, with a five-year vesting schedule. When the first year elapses, the stock price is at $11. You decide to exercise 20,000 shares, which will cost you $200,000, exceeding the $100,000 limit. Thus, $100,000 will be considered ISOs and the remaining $100,000 would be nonquals. As a rule of thumb, for any given year, up to $100,000 of the exercise amount that vests will be treated as an ISO. Any amount that vests above this will be treated as a nonqual.

The Super Stock Option

WHEN 401(K)S AND EMPLOYEE stock ownership plans (ESOPs) started to become a big part of executive compensation, Congress wanted to offer rank-and-file employees the opportunity to participate in these benefits. Currently, Congress is considering new legislation called the Wealth through the Workplace Act (HR 3462).

If the legislation passes, it would create a "super stock option." To implement this type of stock option, employers must have at least 70 percent of employees participate in the plan, which applies only to options based on publicly traded stocks or stocks traded through in-house exchanges.

The super stock option combines the benefits of ISOs and non-quals. For example, the options can be priced at 85 percent of the fair market value of the stock price. No taxes apply when the option is exercised, and the tax structure is the same as if the option were an ISO.

Disqualifying Disposition

A DISQUALIFYING DISPOSITION OCCURS when you exercise your options and then sell stock before you are eligible to receive favorable tax treatment. Instead of being taxed at capital gains rates, you are taxed at ordinary income rates.

Suppose your company grants you 5,000 ISOs with an exercise price of $10 per share and a vesting schedule that lasts five years. One year later, you decide to exercise 1,000 options.

But in order to get ISO status on the sale of the stock, you must hold on to your ISO options for at least two years from the date of the option grant and at least one year from the date of the option exercise. If you hold your 1,000 options for an extra year, you will meet the holding requirement, and the sale will be subject to capital gains treatment.

Let's continue the example from above. You own 1,000 shares of XYZ, exercised at $10 per share. You did not incur any taxes under the regular tax system when you exercised the shares. The stock price is currently $20.

You wait another year after the exercise and then sell the 1,000 shares for $30 each. Since you recognized no taxes at the time of the exercise, your basis is the exercise amount, which was $10,000 ($10 times 1,000 shares). The gain on the transaction is $20,000 ($30,000 for the sale minus the $10,000 basis). Since you met the holding period, the $20,000 gain is taxed at the long-term capital gains rate of 20 percent. So your taxes are $4,000.

Now let's change the facts so we can look at this another way. Suppose the company allowed you to exercise your options early, and after six months of the grant, you exercised 1,000 shares. Then you held on to the shares for one year.

In this case, part of the transaction would be taxed as a capital gain and part as ordinary income. First of all, you would have a long-term capital gain on the difference between the sales price of the stock and the fair market value of the stock on the date of exercise. Next, you would owe ordinary income taxes on the difference between the fair market value of the stock at exercise and the fair market value of the stock at the time of the grant. This would be considered a disqualifying disposition. So the capital gain would be $20,000, and the gain subject to the ordinary income tax rate would be $10,000.

After the exercise, you sell the ISO shares within one year. This transaction would be considered a short-term capital gain and subject to ordinary income tax rates. Basically, the complete transaction would be a disqualifying disposition and taxed completely at ordinary income tax rates. That is, it would be as if you had exercised a nonqual.

Besides a sale of stock, other ways you can trigger a disqualifying disposition include the following:

➢ using your ISO shares to exercise other ISO shares
➢ transferring shares to an irrevocable trust. This is a disqualifying disposition because you cannot take back your shares.
➢ gifting shares to someone other than a spouse
➢ the short sale of your stock

Note that the following situations do *not* give rise to a disqualifying disposition:

➤ transfer because of the option holder's death
➤ transferring shares to a revocable trust (unlike an irrevocable trust, you can take back your shares)
➤ transferring stock to a stockbroker
➤ using stock as collateral to borrow money (although if the stock is sold because you must meet a margin call, then there is a disposition)
➤ transfer of stock into joint tenancy
➤ conversion of the stock from common to preferred or vice versa
➤ transfer because of a divorce
➤ transfer that is the result of a bankruptcy

Note: Most people do not deal with estimated tax payments because their employers automatically withhold taxes from their paychecks. But if you have ISO income, you will likely have to pay quarterly estimated taxes (for 2000, payments were due on April 17, June 15, September 15, and January 16). If you do not make these payments, you are subject to a penalty, which is interest on the amount owed.

Essentially, you must pay estimated tax if your withholding does not cover 90 percent of your current tax liability. But there are exceptions if (a) your withholding and tax credits equal at least your prior year's tax liability or (b) the amount due, after subtracting withholding and credits, is less than $1,000.

Unfortunately, tax treatment of ISOs is much more complex than that of nonquals, because ISOs are subject to the alternative minimum tax (AMT).

Alternative Minimum Tax

THERE ARE REALLY TWO TAX SYSTEMS: the regular one and the alternative minimum tax (AMT). The AMT tax system excludes a variety of deductions that the regular tax system allows. Why? Well, Congress wanted to make sure that wealthy individuals paid their fair share of taxes. Unfortunately, AMT does not hit only the rich. In fact, it is becoming more common for middle-class workers to be subject to AMT, largely because of ISOs. Whenever an ISO is exercised, AMT is triggered, with one exception: if you sell the stock in the same year you exercised the ISO, you will not have any AMT consequences.

If you do trigger this penalty, you must calculate your taxes based on the regular system as well as the AMT. Then you must pay the higher amount.

Let's look at the process. First of all, let's calculate taxes under the regular system. With your CPA, you begin the process of filling out your 1040 form. You had total income of $100,000 last year. As you know, you can make adjustments to the total income. Adjustments are tax deductions, which are available to you whether you elect to take itemized deductions or the standard deduction. These adjustments include IRA contributions, alimony, and student loan interest. Suppose you had $5,000 in adjustments. You subtract this from $100,000, and the result is $95,000, which is called your adjusted gross income.

Next, you need to decide if you want to itemize your deductions or take the standard deduction. Of course, you calculate both and select the one that has the highest tax savings. When using itemized deductions, you can deduct such things as mortgage interest, local taxes, and medical expenses. With the standard deduction, this is a fixed amount. You decide to itemize your deductions, which gives you $15,000 in deductions. The income subject to taxation is $80,000.

But there is more. You get a personal exemption, which amounts to $2,800. There are also personal exemptions allowed for all your dependents. You have one child. Therefore, you can take your personal exemption, the exemption for your spouse, and an exemption for your child. The exemptions total $8,400. This is subtracted from $80,000, which equals $71,600. This amount is your taxable income. You then apply your tax rate. If it is 35 percent, then your income taxes will be $25,060.

In addition, you may have tax credits, which are applied to the taxes you pay. Tax credits are allowed for such things as child care, as well as for the exercise of stock options for AMT purposes. If your tax credit is $10,000, then you owe $15,060 ($25,060 minus $10,000). In fact, if the tax credit is more than the taxes you owe, then you receive a refund for the balance. For example, if you have a $30,000 tax credit, then you receive a refund of $4,940.

Now let's calculate the AMT. To do so, you need to fill out Form 6251, Alternative Minimum Tax—Individuals. The instructions on the form are easy to understand and enlightening. Essentially, the form takes your adjusted gross income from your 1040, which is $95,000. Form 6251 will make adjustments from the gross adjusted income. After the adjustments are made, the resulting figure is the alternative minimum taxable income (AMTI). The adjustments can be positive or negative. They include the following:

➤ **Tax-exempt interest.** Municipal bonds are a common way investors receive tax-exempt interest. In fact, many wealthy people use municipal bonds to shelter their income.

➤ **Tax shelters.** Since the late 1980s, the government has been severely cutting back on tax shelters. However, there are still some left, including certain partnerships.

➤ **Interest on second mortgages.** If you borrow against your home for purposes other than financing your home, there may be AMT consequences.

➤ **State and local taxes.** Many taxpayers deduct these expenses as itemized deductions. But they can result in AMT consequences.

➤ **Miscellaneous itemized deductions.** These are deductions that are allowed on your tax return if they are 2 percent or more of your adjusted gross income. But if the amounts are much higher, you could incur the AMT.

Once the AMTI is computed, it is reduced by an exemption of $33,750 for singles, $45,000 for married persons, and $22,500 for married persons filing separate returns. Unfortunately, the exemption is phased out based on your income. Here are the phaseout ranges:

➤ $112,500 to $247,500 AMTI for single persons
➤ $150,000 to $330,000 for married persons
➤ $75,000 to $165,000 for married persons filing separately

After netting out the exemptions, you multiply the resulting amount by the AMT rate. AMT rates are 26 percent for AMTI of up to $175,000 and 28 percent for AMTI above $175,000. However, any capital gains are still taxed at a maximum of 20 percent.

When you exercise your options, there is no definitive way to know if you owe the AMT. The tax year must be completed in order for you to assess your overall tax situation. Thus, it is critical to find a top-notch CPA to handle the complex tax issues. See Chapter 11 for some additional information on finding an accountant.

Remember, this discussion covers the AMT for federal taxes. If your state has an income tax system, it may also have its own AMT system. Any state taxes—including state AMT—count as a deduction on your federal return, as long as you itemize. However, if you are subject to federal AMT, you cannot deduct any state taxes.

It is important to seek the counsel of a CPA to find out if you can change the time you pay your state AMT (that is, shift it to another year). If this is possible, you may be able to lower your federal AMT burden.

An AMT Transaction

TWO YEARS AGO, YOUR COMPANY granted you options to purchase 5,000 shares at $10 each. The vesting period is four years. Last year, you exercised 1,000 shares. At that time, the stock price was $15. Currently, the stock price is $20, and you decide to sell the shares. Since you have met the holding period, the transaction is treated as an ISO.

For the regular tax system, you have a capital gain of $10,000. The tax would be $2,000 (20 percent times $10,000).

However, waiting for the holding period to elapse can be a risky strategy. After all, the company may experience troubles that could make the stock plunge. If the stock falls back to $10 per share, then you would have no gain on the transaction.

If your stock fell to $5 per share, you would then have a capital loss of $5,000 ($5 times 1,000 shares), which is calculated as $5,000 minus the $10,000 cost basis. As discussed in the last chapter, you can offset the $5,000 loss against other capital gains. If there is not enough to satisfy the loss, you can deduct $3,000 in net losses. This is known as the capital loss limitation.

In these examples, an AMT adjustment occurred. This was equal to the gain at the time of the exercise, which was $10,000. Depending on your overall tax situation, you may have had to pay the AMT tax for the year you exercised the options.

So let's say you owed $30,000 in AMT for the current tax year. But in the following tax year, you do not owe any AMT. Actually, you can use the $10,000 AMT adjustment as a tax credit. For example, if you owe $15,000 in federal income taxes, you can apply the AMT as a tax credit and pay only $5,000 in taxes. Keep in mind that you can use the AMT tax credit only for years in which you do not owe the AMT. You can do this by filling out Form 8801, Credit for Prior Year Minimum Tax—Individuals, Estates, and Trusts.

A year after you exercised the 1,000 ISOs, you sold 1,000 shares, so this year, you do owe AMT. You will need to calculate the capital gain on the sale of the shares. However, you will compute an AMT basis by adding the AMT adjustment to the exercise amount. This would be $30,000 (the $20,000 exercise amount plus the AMT adjustment of $10,000). In fact, if the stock is selling, say, at $25 per share, you will be subject to a capital gain of $5,500 per share.

Share Exchanges

AS WITH NONQUALS, YOU MAY have difficulty finding the money to exercise your stock options. One consideration that makes a big difference—at least in terms of taxes—is the type of stock you use in the exchange. As a general rule, it is better not to use immature stock. Immature stock is stock you have acquired in an exercise that did not meet the ISO holding requirement.

You will have better results if the stock you use for the exchange is mature stock (which meets the holding requirement), stock purchased on the open market, or stock that was acquired through a nonqualified stock option.

Example: You have options to buy 5,000 shares at an exercise price of $5 per share. The vesting schedule is five years. The current stock price is $10 per share, and you already own 4,000 shares, which are not immature. To exercise the 1,000 shares that have vested, you will exchange 500 of the shares you already own. This is equal to $5,000, which is the exercise amount. In the transaction, the 500 shares you traded are called the exchange shares. The 500 shares that you gained from the exercise of the option are called the additional shares.

Since this is an exercise of an ISO option, there are no tax consequences for the regular federal income tax system. The 500 exchange shares have the same basis as the shares you turned in, as well as the same holding period for determining whether the shares qualify for ISO status. The added shares have a basis that is equal to the cash you paid to exercise the option. In this case, you did not pay any cash, so the basis is zero. The ISO holding period for these shares begins on the exercise of the ISO option.

What about the AMT? Well, when you exercise the 1,000 ISO options, you will report an adjustment for the AMT as if you paid cash for the shares. The AMT basis for the exchange shares will be equal to the exercise amount of $2,500 ($5 exercise price times 500 shares). The AMT basis for the added shares is equal to the cash you paid plus the AMT adjustment.

If you use immature ISO shares to do the exchange, you do not recognize any taxes for the regular federal tax system, but on the other hand, the transaction will be treated as a disqualifying disposition. That is, you will recognize ordinary income from the old option that was the basis of the shares you used for the exchange.

The exchange shares have the same basis as the shares you turned in, plus the amount of compensation income you reported as a result of the disqualifying disposition. What's more, the exchange shares have the same holding period for determining long-term capital gains as the shares that were turned in. As for the holding period for determining the ISO status, this begins when you exercise the new ISO.

The added shares have as a basis any cash you paid for the stock. The holding period for long-term capital gains and ISO status begins on the date of exercise of the new ISO.

Timing

WHEN DOING TAX PLANNING, timing is critical. There are some useful strategies to keep in mind when dealing with ISOs.

One approach is to exercise your options when the value of the stock plunges. On the surface, this sounds easy, but timing the stock market can be very difficult. Take a look at PlanetRX, an online medical site. The company went public in October 1999 and reached $24.50. Then the stock declined to $14.50 by December. Good time to exercise? No way. By April 2000, the stock was at $3. Now it trades at 10¢.

Another strategy revolves around the capital loss limitation. As mentioned previously, you can deduct only $3,000 in net losses for AMT purposes. This can mean paying large amounts of taxes even if your gains are small. The best strategy here is to exercise your options early in the year.

Example: A year ago, your company, XYZ, granted you options for 10,000 shares. The stock has soared, and your options are worth $400,000. You exercise the 10,000 shares at the beginning of the year, which gives you an AMT adjustment of $400,000.

Unfortunately, XYZ's stock plunges, and by the end of the year, the value of your holdings is only $20,000. If you do not sell the stock, you will owe $112,000 in AMT.

True, you will be able to recover part of the AMT in the next tax year through the AMT credit, but the amount is very small. It is the gain on the stock (for federal tax purposes) plus $3,000, which is the capital loss limitation amount, a total of $23,000. In other words, your net tax bill is $77,000 even though the gain on your stock was only $20,000.

To avoid this situation, you could have sold your shares before the year ended. In this case, you would not have been subject to AMT. Rather, you would have paid ordinary income taxes on your $20,000 gain.

Early Exercise—83(b) Election

YOUR EMPLOYER MAY ALLOW you to exercise your ISOs early. This can not only help you comply with the holding period requirements but also reduce your AMT exposure. But as with a nonqual, you need to make an 83(b) election to get these benefits.

For example, your employer, XYZ, grants you ISO options on 10,000 shares. The exercise price is $1 per share, and the fair market value is $1 per share. There is an early-exercise provision. You exercise the 10,000 shares by paying $10,000. Since you have no gain on this transaction, the preference item for AMT is zero.

Consider the Big Picture

IN MANY CASES OPTION HOLDERS focus mostly on the tax consequences of their options, but this can undermine long-term financial planning goals. For example, keeping your ISOs long enough to meet the holding requirement sounds like a great strategy, except for an interesting wrinkle: the difference in the tax rates between AMT (28 percent maximum) and long-term capital gains (20 percent maximum).

To illustrate, let's suppose you exercise your shares and you have a gain of $100,000. As a result, you must pay $28,000 in AMT. You sell the shares and receive a long-term capital gain of $20,000. In this case, you can use only $20,000 of your AMT credit for the year in which you pay the capital gains. The remaining $8,000 can be used for the following years. Or, worse, if your stock plunges, you may have to pay taxes that exceed the gain on your stock.

In other words, when planning your stock option strategies, you need to consider your complete financial situation and all the potential consequences of your decisions. In such cases, a CPA or financial planner can be a tremendous help in evaluating the pros and cons of each approach. For more information on selecting these advisers, see Chapter 11.

Chapter Four

Nonqualified Stock Options

I F A STOCK OPTION PLAN does not meet the Internal Revenue Code's requirements for an incentive stock option plan, then by default it is a nonqualified stock option plan (nonqual). Sometimes referred to as NQOs or NQSOs, nonquals do not provide any special tax treatments for holders. Nonquals can be granted to employees and to nonemployees, including independent contractors, directors, attorneys, private investors (such as venture capitalists), and consultants.

At the time of grant, there is typically no taxable gain, even though there may be instances in which a nonqual is substantially "in the money" at the time of grant. Let's say you get a 10,000-share option grant with an exercise price of $5, and the current market price is $20. The options are $15 in the money and would likely be considered taxable, but not from the time you were given the grant. Rather, you recognize income from a nonqual when you exercise the option.

The gain is equal to the difference between the fair market value of the stock and the exercise price of the option. This spread is often called the "bargain element." Thus, the mere act of exercising the option creates a taxable gain, as shown by the table on the following page.

By contrast, the exercise of an ISO does not in itself create a taxable gain, though it may trigger the alternative minimum tax.

Example: You have nonqualified options on 10,000 shares of XYZ

Taxes on 1,000 Shares at an Exercise Price of $10 per Share

TAXES	ISO	NQSO	SUPER STOCK OPTION
Employee exercises when market value is $20 per share	No tax paid	Tax = ($20 - $10)* 1,000*(0.28) = $2,800	No tax paid
Employee sells at $30 per share after holding 1 year or more	($30 - $10)* 1,000*(0.20) = $4,000	($30 - $20)* 1,000* (0.20) = $2,000	($30 - $10)* 1,000 (0.20) = $4,000
Total tax paid	$4,000	$4,800	$4,000

Source: Salary.com. Assumes an ordinary income tax rate of 28 percent. The capital gains tax rate is 20 percent.

Co., and those options have vested. The exercise price is $20, and the fair market value of each share is $30. You exercise the options on 10,000 shares, thus purchasing them for $200,000. You now are considered to have taxable income of $100,000, which is the difference between the fair market value ($300,000) and the exercise purchase amount. The $100,000 gain is part of your gross income; in other words, it is as if you had been paid $100,000 in wages for the year. If you are in the 39.5 percent tax bracket, your tax bill will be $39,500.

If the company is traded on a public exchange, then the fair market value is usually the average between the high and low price for the day on which the option was exercised. For the stock of a private company, the fair market value has to be estimated by an independent appraiser, an investment adviser, or even the company itself.

If you are an employee, then your employer will withhold taxes from your wages in order to cover the taxes that will be due on the $100,000 bargain element (directors and consultants usually are not considered employees). Thus, even though $100,000 of your compensation was in discounted stock, you will need to pay your taxes with cash. If your wages do not cover the amount to be withheld, you have to come up with the money to pay the tax to your employer, who then pays the tax to the government. This amount is put on your W-2 Form.

In rare cases, your company may help you pay this tax, but its payment is also considered income and is itself subject to withholding taxes. Also, some people will use the stock purchased as collateral for a loan to pay for the withholding tax.

If you are not an employee, there is no withholding requirement, but that merely means that you must pay self-employment tax, as well as federal and state taxes, yourself. This income is reported not on your W-2 but on Form 1099-Misc.

You may have a large amount of nonquals. If so, keep in mind that if you exercise all of them during the same year, you might have to pay a large amount of tax. That's why it is important to plan such cash-flow issues before exercising the options.

After you pay taxes on your $100,000 gain, any subsequent gains on the shares are treated as capital gains when you sell them. This means you must keep track of the cost basis of your shares. The basis is equal to the amount you paid for the exercise of the options plus the gain you realized. In our example above, your cost basis would be $300,000, which is the $200,000 exercise amount plus the $100,000 gain on which you've already paid taxes. Suppose that the stock rises to $35 per share from $30. You sell your 10,000 shares and receive $350,000. Subtract from this amount the cost basis of $300,000, and your capital gain is $50,000.

If the sale occurs sooner than twelve months from the time of the exercise, the $50,000 is considered a short-term capital gain, with a tax rate of up to 39.9 percent. Otherwise, the transaction is a long-term capital gain, and the tax rate is 20 percent. See the table on the following page for a comparison of the tax implications of different classes of stock options.

Note: In certain instances you do not recognize income when you exercise nonquals. This occurs if, at the time of the exercise, the stock acquired is subject to a substantial risk of forfeiture and is not transferable. When either of these conditions no longer applies, you must recognize the ordinary income on the stock.

Let's take a closer look at this:

1   **Substantial risk of forfeiture.** This means the employer has the right to revoke the stock options before they vest. As an example, you receive options on 10,000 shares of your company, of which 5,000 vest after one year and the remaining 5,000 vest after two

Taxes Implications of Three Types of Stock Options

TAXES	ISO	NQSO	SUPER STOCK OPTION
Employee exercises options	No tax paid	Ordinary income tax (28%–39.6%)	No tax
Employee gets tax deduction?	No deduction	Tax deduction upon employee exercise	Tax deduction upon employee exercise
Employee sells options after 1 year or more	Long-term capital gains tax at 20%	Long-term capital gains tax at 20%	Long-term capital gains tax at 20%

Source: Salary.com.

years. The exercise price is $5 per share. According to your options contract, you are allowed to exercise the 10,000 options at the time you receive them. However, this particular option contract also gives the employer the right to terminate your employment and revoke your stock options. The company would do this by repurchasing your 10,000 shares at $5 apiece. Because of this possibility, your options under this contract have a "substantial risk of forfeiture."

2 **Not transferable.** Stock that is acquired upon exercise of a nonqualified stock option is transferable. The exception is if the option contract or other agreement specifically provides otherwise. Also, the "short-swing" profit recapture rule, part of the federal securities laws, prevents insiders of public companies from making profits on purchases and sales of stock held for less than six months. This effectively makes an insider's stock options nontransferable for tax law purposes.

Let's look at the two rules above in action. You are granted an option to purchase 20,000 shares of XYZ, a public company. The exercise price is $10 per share. The first 10,000 shares vest after one year, and the remaining 10,000 shares vest after two years. A year goes by, and you exercise the first 10,000 shares at the current fair market price of $20.

In the meantime, you have been promoted to the post of vice president of marketing, so you are now considered an insider. As a result, you are subject to the short-swing rule. If you had also purchased stock in the market three months ago (note that the option exercise is not a "purchase" under these rules), you could not take a profit on your 10,000 shares, and you meet the requirements of a substantial risk of forfeiture (that is, if you sell within three months, you must give back your profits). So at the time of the exercise, no income is recognized. Instead, the income is recognized after three months, when the short-swing rule no longer applies.

Cashless Exercise

COMING UP WITH THE TAX MONEY for the exercise of your stock options may be difficult. If so, you may want to consider the "cashless exercise" mentioned in the previous chapter. This maneuver is typically done through a broker who has a relationship with the employer. Before doing the cashless exercise, you need to establish a cash and margin account with the firm. You need a margin account because the broker will use your options as collateral when taking a loan to purchase the shares.

Here is how it works: You have options on 10,000 shares of your company, and those options have vested. The exercise price is $20, and the fair market value of each share is $30. The broker will put up the $10,000, enabling you to exercise the options and then sell the acquired stock on the open market for $300,000. A commission of perhaps $500 is deducted. You will thus get net proceeds of $99,500 ($300,000 sales price, minus the purchase of the stock for $200,000, minus the commission of $500). There is no interest on the loan.

This pair of transactions is usually done on a single day; in fact, the transaction is often referred to as a "same day" sale. In this sale, you may actually have a capital gain or loss, apart from the bargain element created by the gap between your exercise price and the market value of the shares. Why? Because the fair market value, as stated above, is usually the average of the high and low price of the day. If the stock dropped a tick in the minutes or seconds you owned it, or if it simply was sold at a price lower than the day's average, then there would be a loss. Such a gain or loss is typically very small.

Option holders typically have some confusion about cashless exercises, because two transactions were involved: the exercise and the sale of the stock. If you are an employee, the gain stemming from the exercise is reported on your W-2. Since you subsequently sold the stock, this is also reported on a 1099-B. Both statements will show the same amount of gain, which is $100,000. But this does not mean you are taxed twice. Rather, the W-2 shows the $100,000 gain as part of your wages, whereas the 1099-B form documents the fact that you sold the stock.

Companies with a large number of employees have difficulties managing the exercise of stock options. To help streamline the process, some companies have set up online exercises. For example, at PeopleSoft, employees have a digital signature (based on a user identification and password) that allows them to exercise options with a click of the mouse. If you want to do a cashless exercise, however, you still need to call the company's affiliate broker and set up the necessary cash and margin accounts.

Using Shares to Exercise Nonquals

YOUR COMPANY MIGHT HAVE a policy that allows you to use shares you already own to exercise stock options and acquire additional shares. As with a cashless exercise, not all companies allow for such stock swaps.

Let's say your options on 10,000 shares of your company have vested. The exercise price is $20, with a fair market value of $50. You also own outright 5,000 shares of XYZ, which have a cost basis of $10 per share.

To exercise the option, you need to come up with $200,000. One way you can pay for the exercise is by turning in to the company the necessary amount of shares. This would be 4,000 shares, which equals $200,000 (4,000 shares times $50 per share). You take these shares from the 5,000 you already own. The company accepts them in lieu of $200,000 cash and issues you 10,000 shares of new stock.

Computing the taxes on this maneuver is somewhat convoluted.

The IRS considers that two transactions took place. First, there is a tax-free exchange of the old shares (the 4,000 you already owned) for the new ones (the 4,000 used for the exercise). So far, you don't owe any taxes. But because you received 10,000 new shares, the IRS says you have gained 6,000 additional shares for no payment. The total value of these shares—$180,000—is considered ordinary income. This is calculated as 6,000 shares times the $30 gain ($50 market value minus the $20 exercise price). Any subsequent gain on the 6,000 shares is considered a capital gain, while any subsequent gain on the other 4,000 shares is based on its original cost basis, which was $10 per share.

Suppose that the 4,000 shares you handed in were from the prior exercise of an incentive stock option. You exercised that option and bought these shares six months ago. You need another six months to get preferential capital gains treatment. If you use these shares for the stock swap, will you lose the ISO treatment? No, because the exchange is not considered a disqualifying disposition.

Unfortunately, things get much more complex when you are using stock other than nonquals to pay for the exercise of an ISO. Three common scenarios are exchanging immature ISOs for ISOs, stock swaps, and reloads.

Exchanging Immature ISOs for ISOs

STOCK YOU HAVE ACQUIRED by the exercise of ISOs but have not held long enough to meet the IRS holding requirement (for having any capital gains considered long-term) are referred to as "immature ISOs." The holding requirements mandate that you hold the stock until the later of either one year after the date you exercised the option or two years after the date you received it.

For example, six months ago you exercised an incentive stock option on XYZ stock and acquired 10,000 shares at an exercise price of $20. You were granted the options one year ago, and now you want to use some of the 10,000 shares to exercise another ISO you have for 1,000 shares with an exercise price of $25 per share. The 10,000 shares are immature on two counts: it has been less than two years since those ISOs were granted, and it is also less than one year since you exercised them. The current fair market value of the stock is $50.

To exercise the 1,000-share ISO, you need to turn in 500 existing immature ISO shares (500 shares times $50).

By turning in the 500 immature ISO shares, you have made a disqualifying disposition. This means you recognize as income the gain you made on those 500 shares when you originally exercised the 10,000-share ISO at $20. At that time, the fair market value of the stock was $30, which means you had a $10 gain. For 500 shares, the total gain would be $5,000 ($10 times 500 shares). In fact, you need to report this gain as ordinary income, even if the current fair market value of the stock is lower.

Next, the transfer of the 500 immature ISO shares for the exercise of the 1,000-share ISO is treated as a tax-free exchange. That is, no taxes are owed. The 500 shares are called exchange shares.

But of the new 1,000 ISO exercise, the remaining 500 shares that are not part of the swap are considered a disqualifying disposition, because these are newly acquired shares and do not meet the IRS holding requirements. These shares are known as added shares. The gain on this transaction would be $12,500. This is calculated as 500 shares times the $25-per-share gain ($50 current fair market value minus the $25 exercise price).

If the 1,000-share ISO had been mature, then there would, of course, have been no disqualifying disposition. Rather, any subsequent sale of the 500 added shares would have been treated as capital gains.

Since the transaction involves ISOs, dual cost basis is involved. Let's first look at cost basis for the regular federal tax.

The cost basis of the exchange shares are equal to the basis of the shares turned in. Since there was a disqualifying disposition, the gain is added to the cost basis. Thus, the cost basis is $10,000, which is equal to the exercise price of $5,000 ($10 times 500) plus the $5,000 gain.

The added shares have a cost basis that is equal to any cash used to pay for the exercise. In this case, shares were used to exercise all 1,000 shares and no cash was used, so the basis is zero.

Now let's take a look at the cost basis for AMT. When you exercised the 1,000 options, you must report an AMT adjustment for the gain, which was $12,500. The added shares have an AMT cost basis equal to the cash you paid for the exercise plus the AMT adjustment.

Since no cash was used, the AMT basis is $12,500. The exchange shares have the same AMT basis as the shares you used to pay for the ISO. This is $6,000.

What about the cost basis for exchanging mature ISOs for mature or immature ISOs? A "mature ISO" is shorthand for ISO stock you have held long enough to satisfy the holding requirement. For example, you exercised an ISO on your company's stock for 5,000 shares more than a year ago, and the ISO was granted to you three years ago, so both the one-year and two-year parts of the holding period are satisfied. The exercise price was $5 per share, and at the time of the exercise you recognized a $5-per-share gain. You want to use some of the 5,000 shares to exercise another ISO for 1,000 shares with an exercise price of $10. The 1,000-share ISO is also mature.

The current market value of XYZ is $20 per share. To come up with the $10,000 you need, you use 500 of your mature ISO shares (at $20 per share) to exercise the 1,000 ISO (at $10 per share).

Again, for the 500 shares you turned in, this is a tax-free exchange. These exchange shares you are acquiring will have the same basis as the stock you turned in. The basis was $5 per share, or a total of $2,500 ($5 exercise price times 500 shares). The 500 added shares have the basis of any cash you used to exercise the ISO. No cash was paid, so the cost basis is zero.

Since you are exercising an ISO, you need to make an AMT adjustment with the 1,000 ISO shares. This is the gain at the time of the exercise, which was $10,000. That amount is equal to the market value, or $20,000 ($20 times 1,000 shares), minus the exercise amount of $10,000.

The exchange shares have the same AMT basis as the shares you used to pay the exercise price, or $5,000. This is equal to the $2,500 (500 times $5) exercise amount plus the $2,500 (500 times $5) gain at the time of the exercise.

Other Stock Swaps

LET'S SAY YOU TRADE IN 1,000 shares of stock in order to exercise 500 shares' worth of nonquals. In the transaction, you have a gain of $25,000. Even though you really have not sold any stock in the sense of turning shares into cash, the IRS still requires that you pay the tax in cash. This is done either as withholding (if you are an employee) or self-employment taxes (if you work for yourself).

What's more, a stock swap can seem cumbersome. In the example above, you are handing over 4,000 shares to get 10,000. Wouldn't it also make sense to keep the 4,000 shares and instead get 6,000 from the exercise? Well, the IRS agrees that there is no real difference. According to the IRS, you must meet certain requirements that verify you own the 4,000 shares. If your shares are in street name, then you need to provide the IRS with a notarized statement from your broker. If you hold the certificates, then you submit the certificate numbers to the IRS.

When doing stock swaps, you need to be aware of the concept of identifying shares. The IRS allows you to specify which shares you want to sell. This can be helpful for your tax planning purposes.

Example: Suppose that about nine months ago, you exercised ISOs on 7,000 shares for $5 each, paying $35,000. Then last month you purchased 5,000 shares of your company's stock for $10 per share, paying a total of $50,000 in cash—no options involved. In all, you have 12,000 shares, of which you decide to sell 4,000.

Unless you specify which shares you want to sell, the IRS will apply the rule of first in, first out (FIFO). In other words, the IRS will consider the transaction to come from the shares resulting from the exercise of the ISO. This would be to your disadvantage, because if you sold the ISO shares, it would be considered a disqualifying disposition and would be taxed as ordinary income. It would make more sense to instead specify 4,000 shares from the 5,000 you just bought.

The IRS gives you the choice of selecting which shares are part of the sale. But you must specify this at the time of the sale. How you do this depends on whether you hold the certificates or your broker holds them in street name. If the certificates are in your possession, then you merely send the ones you want to specify to the transfer agent. The transfer agent is a firm that handles the transfer of stock certificates when a trade is made. Make sure the broker understands why it matters that the right shares are sold.

If the certificates are in street name, notify your broker which shares you want to sell when you are ready to proceed. Be very clear about this, and state the exact date on which you bought the shares.

You will then receive a written confirmation of the specification from your broker. If you do not, ask for it. Without the confirmation, there might be no proof of the specification.

What if you are using an Internet broker? How do you specify which shares you want to sell? If the broker has an 800 number, then you can call and have the broker send a confirmation. If not, you can send an e-mail and request that the broker send back a written confirmation.

Reloads

A RELOAD IS NOT THE SAME as a stock swap. It is a feature that gives you an extra benefit whenever you do a swap. A reload allows you to use stock you own to exercise an option and also to get a new option. The new option has an exercise price equal to the current fair market value of the stock. A reload is a feature that would be specified in your option agreement.

For example, suppose that you own 10,000 shares of XYZ stock. The current fair market value of the stock is $20. You also have an option to buy 1,000 shares with an exercise price of $8. The option has a reload feature.

You use 400 shares' worth to exercise the 1,000-share option, which has a purchase price of $8,000 (1,000 shares times $8 per share). You will get a new option for 400 shares at the current fair market value of $20 per share. This is your reload. Since you are receiving only the option to buy 400 shares at the current fair market value, there is no taxable gain recognized at the time the reload is granted.

To understand the reload feature, read your option contract carefully. Some reloads allow you to use only shares you have owned for a certain period of time for the exercise. Or the company might require that you use shares that you gained from a prior option exercise.

83(b) Election

WHEN YOU WORK FOR a private company, there could be serious adverse tax consequences for nonquals. The main reason is that the private company may experience a huge appreciation in value while you are waiting for the nonquals to vest, which could result in a large tax liability for you on the vesting date of your options.

For instance, two years ago you joined a start-up company. After the first year, you had a stock option that vested for 6,000 shares at 50¢ per share. You exercised the option. At the time, the stock price of XYZ was $1 per share. However, the 6,000 shares were restricted and subject to forfeiture for one year.

Six months after the exercise, the company goes public. The stock price is now $50 per share. Since you hold nonquals, you must recognize income when you exercise your 6,000 shares. The gain is $49.90 per share, or $299,400. Assuming your tax rate is 39.9 percent, the tax bill will be $119,460.

But you can deal with this problem by using an 83(b) election. Here's how it works: When you get the 6,000 options, you exercise all of them, which costs $3,000 (6,000 shares times 50¢). You then file an 83(b) election with the IRS within thirty days of the exercise. As a result, you pay ordinary income taxes on $3,000, even though the stock is restricted and subject to forfeiture. Assuming a 39.9 percent tax rate, the tax bill is $1,197. Now, any subsequent gain on the stock is treated as a capital gain, which typically is more advantageous than paying ordinary income taxes. So instead of paying taxes at 39.9 percent, you would be paying at a maximum tax rate of 20 percent, provided you hold on to the stock for more than one year.

However, you do run some risks with an 83(b) filing. For example, what if the company goes bankrupt and the shares are worthless? In this case, it would not make sense to exercise the options, since they have no value. In other words, you may have paid taxes for no reason at all.

There is also the risk of forfeiture. You might be fired, and in this case, the stock will be repurchased from you at the price you paid for the exercise. If this is the case, the basis of the stock is the exercise price. You do not get to add to the basis any of the tax you paid.

As an example, let's say you are granted an option to purchase 10,000 XYZ shares for $1 per share. All shares vest in one year. You exercise the options at $1 and make an 83(b) election. The current market price is $1.50, so you have a gain of $5,000, on which you pay ordinary income taxes. Before one year passes, you are terminated, and XYZ repurchases your shares for $1 each. The basis of the stock is $1, so you do not have to pay any taxes on the transac-

A Sample 83(b) Statement

UNDER INTERNAL REVENUE Code Section 83(b), I hereby include in gross income, as compensation for services, the excess of the fair market value on the date of transfer of property that I received from XYZ Corp. over the amount I paid for such property.

Taxpayer name: Jane Doe

Address: 1526 Brookhollow #82, Santa Ana, CA 92705

Social Security Number: 111-11-1111

Date of property transfer: January 1, 2000

Description of the property: 10,000 shares of XYZ Corporation common stock acquired by exercising a nonqualified stock option

Amount paid for the stock: $10,000

Taxable year for which election is made: Calendar year 2000

Nature of restriction: Until January 1, 2001, XYZ Corp. has the right to repurchase my stock at the exercise price of $1 per share

Fair market value of the stock on the date of transfer: $1 per share

I have provided copies of this statement as required in the regulation.

tion. But you are out the tax on that $5,000 you never saw.

Note: When you exercise your options to purchase restricted stock, you do not have any rights to transfer the stock acquired. For that reason, most companies will require that you put the stock in an escrow account. Once the stock vests, it is released from the account.

The process of filing an 83(b) election is as follows. First, you need three copies of a written statement consenting to the election. The IRS has no standard forms, so you need to make your own (see the sample statement above).

One copy must go to the IRS within thirty days of the exercise. Next, you must file the second copy with your tax return in the tax year for which you exercised your options. Finally, you must give a copy to your employer. Request a confirmation that the election statement was received. It is best to send all of these statements via certified mail.

The 83(b) statement must contain the following:

➤ your name, address, and Social Security number
➤ the amount you paid for the stock
➤ the restrictions on your stock
➤ the fair market value of the stock at the time you received the grant
➤ the date you received the grant and the taxable year you are making the election. This is usually for the year you were granted the stock, unless you file taxes based on a fiscal year.
➤ the sentence "I have provided copies of this statement as required in the regulation." That is, you filed the statement with the IRS and your employer.

Remember: When you make an 83(b) election, it is irrevocable. You cannot rescind it.

Chapter 5 *Five*

Federal Securities Laws

S INCE STOCK OPTIONS INVOLVE the potential ownership of stock in a company, federal securities laws come into play. These laws can be very complex, but if you do not comply with them, the consequences can be extreme, including fines and even prison. The regulatory obstacle course offers all kinds of potential problems.

Of course, you should consult closely with your advisers on stock ownership issues, but it's a good idea to know the basics. There are two main federal statutes that apply to stock options:

1   **Securities Act of 1933.** This act requires that before securities are offered or sold, they must be registered with the SEC, unless an exemption applies.
2   **Securities Exchange Act of 1934.** This involves a myriad of rules regarding disclosure of stock transactions by executive officers.

Insiders

AN "INSIDER" IS DEFINED IN Section 16 of the Securities Exchange Act of 1934 as anyone who is an officer, director, or owner of 10 percent or more of any class of stock of a public company. An insider is considered to own securities that are actually held by relatives, such as spouses, children, grandchildren, parents, grandparents, and siblings. This means that trades made by such people may be attributed to the insider.

If you are an insider, then special regulations apply to your stock options, including the following reporting requirements.

Reporting Requirements

TRANSACTIONS INVOLVING STOCK OPTIONS must be filed with the SEC. Within ten days of becoming a director or officer of a public company, you are required to file a Form 3. This shows how much stock you own at the date you assume office. Also, you must file this form if your holdings exceed 10 percent of any class of the company's stock.

Over time, you probably will exercise and sell shares. Whenever there is a change in ownership, an insider must file a Form 4. This is done on the tenth day following the end of the month in which the change occurred. Even if there is not a net difference in ownership (for example, you buy 100 shares and sell 100 shares), you still must file a Form 4, unless an exception applies. Changes in ownership also include gifts, transfers to trusts, and stock option exercises. In special circumstances, such as death and divorce, the filing can be deferred, sometimes until the end of the year.

Finally, insiders must file a Form 5 on or before the forty-fifth day after the end of a company's fiscal year. This reports any transactions that were not reported in a Form 4. These may include deferments (for death or divorce) or cases in which the insider simply may have forgotten to file a Form 4.

Keep in mind that you are generally not required to make a report to the SEC when your options are canceled or when they vest.

These disclosures are tedious and may seem to have little significance if, for example, you exercise only 100 shares. But the SEC does not take a lenient view of noncompliance, no matter how trivial the transaction appears to be. There may be fines for noncompliance, and your company may terminate you because of it. In other words, report everything.

The reason for such stringent disclosure rules is that insiders are presumed to be privy to critical information about the company that could result in lucrative trading opportunities. To level the playing field, the SEC requires the disclosure of all stock transactions.

Insider Information

IT MAY SEEM THAT ONLY the brilliant and notorious of Wall Street—such as Ivan Boesky—engage in insider trading. In reality, many ordinary people do so without realizing it.

Insider trading is delineated in Rule 10b-5 in the Securities Exchange Act of 1934 (known as the "antifraud prohibition"). It is defined as trading on the basis of material information that has not been released to the public. What is "material" information? A conservative answer is any information you have that the general public does not—information that can affect the stock price, and thus your own financial position, if you act on what you know. This could include facts about any of these events:

➤ mergers, acquisitions, or joint ventures
➤ management changes
➤ operating or financial results
➤ new products or patents
➤ award of major sales contracts
➤ write-offs
➤ litigation
➤ product delays
➤ stock split

For the most part, insider trading is invoked when an individual purchases or sells securities. Therefore, being granted options or having them vest is not enough to meet the definition. You need either to purchase the underlying securities or sell them to be subject to insider trading rules. But if you are privy to insider information and then pass it on to others (known as "tipping"), you have violated federal securities laws.

Interestingly enough, insider trading rules are based on whether you merely possess the information, not whether it can be proved that the information was the reason behind your trade. Thus, if you sell the stock for other reasons, it would still be considered insider trading. For instance, let's say that you know your company will post strong earnings. You want to sell some of your stock to purchase a new house, and you would have done this regardless of the announcement. Unfortunately, any selling that you do after the earnings report would still be considered insider trading.

In order to reduce the chances of this kind of trouble, many companies will have regular blackout periods during which insiders are prevented from making any transactions. Blackout periods typically are in effect from fifteen days before until two to three days after the announcement of the company's quarterly results.

Your employer is supposed to notify you when the blackout periods occur. If you are contemplating buying or selling shares, though, it doesn't hurt to check with the company's benefits department to be sure.

If you do engage in a prohibited transaction, don't think the SEC will ignore it, even if it is small. In fact, the SEC can be very vigilant against these transactions, in order to set an example for others who might be contemplating insider trading.

To be safe, wait three days after the material information has been announced to the public. This seems like a long time, but you do not want to have any doubt about your transaction. The scope of the SEC's scrutiny can be devastating. If you are caught violating insider trading regulations, you will be liable to the federal government for the profits of the illegal transaction. The penalty may be as much as three times this amount. The criminal violations include prison sentences of up to ten years and fines of up to $1 million.

The securities laws also give the federal government the power to prevent insider traders from becoming corporate officers or directors in the future. Or if you are allowed to assume such a position, you must disclose your violations for future IPO registrations and other corporate disclosure filings with the SEC. Prior violations may make companies reluctant to hire you for top-level positions.

Chat Rooms

ONLINE CHAT ROOMS ARE POPULAR on the Internet, as they allow people to make comments on individual stocks. If your company is public, the chances are great that it is being discussed on investor chat sites.

As an employee, you should refrain from participating in these chats. Especially as a stock-option recipient, you may be privy to insider information, so you risk violating the securities laws by inadvertently tipping on that basis alone. Recently, the SEC set up Cyber Force, a special group of about sixty enforcement lawyers who log on to online chat rooms and discussion groups to find violators of securities laws. In addition to violating securities laws, speaking your mind online can expose you to charges of defamation, theft of trade secrets, and breach of contract.

It is also a bad idea to make comments on competing companies. A company may terminate your employment and your options along with it if you engage in discussions of the company on chat sites. But this is not to imply that you should refrain from reading chats about your company. In fact, monitoring these conversations can be a way for you to gauge the general public sentiment for your company's stock.

Short-Swing Rule

ANOTHER REGULATION DESIGNED to deny insiders the advantage of trading on privileged information is the short-swing rule. Basically, any insider who sells company stock six months before or after acquiring it must return any profits to the company, if at least one of the transactions occurred while the company was public.

For example, say you are an insider and purchased 1,000 shares of your company, which is private, two years ago. The price was $100 per share. Two months ago, you sold the shares for $10,000. There is no liability under the short-swing rule. Now the company goes public. After two months, the stock tumbles. You then buy 1,000 shares for $1,000. The short-swing rule applies because you purchased and sold the stock within six months and generated a profit of $9,000, which must be returned to the company.

However, the grant or exercise of a stock option does not constitute a purchase for the short-swing rule—as long as the grant was approved by the company's board of directors or compensation committee. But beware: the sale of any stock from the exercise will be matched by any shares you purchased in the open market.

To illustrate, say you purchased 500 shares of your company for $10 each. Two months later, you do a cashless exercise of 1,000 shares of company stock. The current fair market value of the stock is $20, and the exercise price was $1. As for your option exercise, 500 shares will be considered a sale for the purposes of the short-swing rule. The profit of $5,000 must be returned to the company ($20 times 500, minus $5,000) for the open-market purchase of its shares.

As a final note on this topic, bona fide gifts are not considered sales for the short-swing rule.

Rule 144

ACCORDING TO THE SECURITIES ACT OF 1933, it is illegal to sell any securities unless you have filed a registration statement with the SEC or an exception applies. The SEC has an exemption for pre-IPO sales by a company to employees (Rule 701). Although this rule also allows employees to sell such stock ninety days after an IPO, most companies have a lockup provision preventing all employees from selling shares within the first six months of the IPO.

But even if the sale is registered, your ability to sell your shares may be limited if you are considered an affiliate of the company. An affiliate is a person with "control" over the company, in the sense of influencing key managerial decisions, or who has access to inside information about the company. Affiliates usually include a company's executive officers and directors and their spouses.

What's more, if the officer or director has a trust that owns more than 10 percent of the total interest of his or her holdings of company stock, then the trustee or executor of that trust would also be considered an affiliate. In fact, anyone who owns at least 10 percent of the outstanding shares of the corporation is considered an affiliate, too.

Don't confuse an affiliate with an "insider," although an affiliate can also be an insider, and an insider can be an affiliate. For example, a director who owns no shares of the company's stock is considered an insider.

So how can an affiliate sell stock? If the stock was not purchased in a registered sale and is thus "restricted," the company can file a special Form S-8 with a resale prospectus to allow the affiliate to sell a stock. An affiliate can also do a private sale, in which case the restrictions pass along to the new owner. Because of this, these sales are often made at steep discounts, and they can become extremely complex.

Alternatively, an affiliate can rely on Rule 144. Under this rule, all stock owned by affiliates is called "control stock." This stock may have been acquired while the company was either public or private. However, shares acquired when the company was private or in an unregistered sale when it is public are called "restricted stock." Restricted stock also can be acquired by gift, inheritance, or divorce.

Before selling restricted stock, an affiliate must own the stock for one year. In other words, the affiliate needs to exercise his or her option and purchase the stock. But this rule does not apply if you sell the stock in a private transaction. Basically, the new buyer will inherit the restrictions that the stock contains.

Because of this, you probably will be forced to sell the securities at a steep discount. In addition, the buyer usually should be a "qualified institutional buyer." Such a buyer is defined as a firm registered under the SEC Act as a securities dealer, investment company, employee benefit plan, or banking institution, or a firm or person that invests, on a regular basis, $100 million in securities of other companies. Finally, some brokerage firms will allow you to borrow against the restricted securities.

If your company is purchased in a merger or acquisition, then the shares you receive may be registered. If so, you can sell them. This also applies if your company is public and you purchased the shares under a stock option or similar plan registered on Form S-8. But Rule 144 has some trading volume restrictions. In any three-month period, the maximum allowed sale is the greater of either (a) 1 percent of the total number of shares outstanding, as last reported, or (b) the average weekly reported volume of trading in the issuer's common stock during the four calendar weeks preceding notice of the sale. These sales include both restricted and unrestricted securities for affiliates. For nonaffiliates, the trading limitations apply to sales made during the first two years after the securities were acquired.

When making a Rule 144 sale, you need to file three copies of Form 144 (Notice of Proposed Sale of Securities Pursuant to Rule 144) with the SEC, and you also must file one copy with the company's stock exchange. This must be done if during the past three months you have sold more than 500 shares or an amount worth more than $10,000.

Key Issues to Consider

➤ If you are an insider (officer, director, or owner of 10 percent of the company), you are subject to a variety of disclosure rules, because you are privy to crucial information about the stock. Disclosures can be tedious, but they are necessary. If you do not comply, you could be fined by the SEC or perhaps even terminated from your position by your employer.

➤ Insider trading is defined as buying or selling stock based on material information that the general public is not aware of. What constitutes insider trading is often not clear. Thus, it is a good idea to talk with your company to see what the insider trading policies are. For example, some companies have "blackout" periods that prevent you from selling stock before certain events, such as the release of quarterly reports.

➤ Even seemingly small violations of insider trading laws can mean big fines and perhaps even a jail sentence.

➤ Chat rooms are becoming a powerful source of investment information. However, it is smart not to participate in chats about your company's stock. You could be liable for violating your company's confidentiality agreements or even insider trading laws.

Section Two

Savvy Negotiations

Evaluating Your Stock Option Contract

O PTION PLANS AND OPTION CONTRACTS are both complex legal documents. When a company initiates an options program, it usually uses a variety of advisers. What's more, it may have more than one option plan, such as one for executives, one for directors, one for consultants, and so on. As discussed in Chapter 11, it is important for you to hire an attorney who specializes in the intricacies of option plans and contracts. This will save you lots of heartache.

Also, when you have negotiated the option contract, make certain that a company officer, such as the CEO or CFO, signs it. If not, the contract may not be valid.

In this chapter, we'll take a look at the crucial clauses in an option contract and show you how to leverage them in your favor.

Offer Letter

AS YOU KNOW, COMPANIES WILL often use a letter to formally offer you a position. If an offer letter is not comprehensive, it will probably be followed up with an official employment agreement. There may also be an employee stock option agreement that goes into further detail. Let's analyze the clauses that you are likely to see in your offer letter or employment agreement.

Start Date

THE START DATE AND ITS DEFINITION should be clearly stated in the contract. Ambiguous dates can cause a great deal of confusion. Is it the date of your hiring? Or is it the start date of the granting or vesting of the stock options? It is very important to make sure these dates are defined in the contract before you sign it. If you are uncertain, go back to the company and ask for clarification on what the start date means for you as an employee and as an option holder. Here's a sample start-date provision:

> This Agreement is made by and between Avanex Corporation (the "Company") and William Lanfri (the "Executive").
>
> Executive's employment with the Company pursuant to this agreement shall commence on June 10, 1998, and continue, if not earlier terminated by either party hereto, until December 18, 1998.

Lanfri signed the agreement on July 17, 1998, as he assumed the role of acting CEO of Avanex, a company that develops high-end equipment for fiber-optic networks. Lanfri's position was interim until a permanent CEO was found.

Duties

MOST EMPLOYMENT CONTRACTS will include some language about your duties as an employee and what the company expects from you. The following is from the employment agreement between FogDog, an online sporting goods store, and Brett Allsop, the president of the company's international division:

> Duties. Executive shall diligently, and to the best of his ability, perform all such duties incident to his position and use his best efforts to promote the interests of the Company.

It is common to see general language for the duties of an employment contract, although there are exceptions. For example, Lanfri, as mentioned earlier, was the acting CEO of his company. Therefore, his contract specified certain goals, such as setting up the Dallas-area office and even interviewing candidates for the permanent CEO position.

If your contract has specific goals, read over the contract carefully and ask yourself whether you are reasonably sure that you can accomplish them. If you do not meet your agreed-on goals, you may be terminated, along with some or all of your stock options.

Option Compensation

HERE IS A GOOD EXAMPLE OF what you might see in an option compensation clause of an employment agreement. This agreement was between Screaming Media, an online software company, and Kevin Clark, the CEO.

> Stock Options. Effective as of the first day of the Term of Employment, the Company shall grant to the Executive a seven-year nonqualified stock option (the "Option") to purchase 450,000 shares of Common Stock of the Company, par value $.01 per share, at an exercise price of $6.50 per share.

The company is granting an option to buy 450,000 shares of Screaming Media at $6.50 per share (the par value of $.01 actually has no bearing on the contract).

Under the Avanex employment contract, Lanfri's option grant was not specified as a number of shares but instead as a percentage:

> Stock Option. The Company will grant to Executive an option for shares of Common Stock equal to 0.75 percent of the Company's outstanding shares of Common Stock on an as-converted and fully diluted basis assuming issuance of all shares of Preferred Stock pursuant to the Series A, Series B, and Series C Preferred Stock Purchase Agreement dated as of February 10, 1998, and at an exercise price of the then fair market value of the Common Stock, as determined by the Board pursuant to a Stock Option Agreement in substantially the form attached hereto as Exhibit A.

Since Avanex is a young company, the number of shares can increase substantially, because the company will go through several more rounds of financing. For each round it will issue a substantial amount of new shares, which can dilute those of earlier shareholders.

The above clause deals with this dilution issue. That is, Lanfri will get 0.75 percent of the company's outstanding shares on a "fully diluted basis." Note that this type of clause is difficult to negotiate, because it is usually reserved for executives with a great deal of leverage.

At-Will Employment

HERE'S A SOBERING CLAUSE from the employment agreement of Bernard Whitney, who was hired as the chief financial officer of Handspring, a developer of handheld computers:

> At-Will Employment. You will be an at-will employee of the Company, which means the employment relationship can be terminated by either of us for any reason at any time. Any statements or representations to the contrary should be regarded by you as ineffective. Further, your participation in any stock option or benefit program is not to be regarded as assuring you of continuing employment for any particular period of time.

An "employment at will" contract can be harsh. This gives your employer the option to terminate your employment at any time, for any reason. This means your options—unvested and perhaps even vested options—can be terminated. The exception, of course, is that you can't be terminated in violation of labor law rights. In other words, the contract would not give the employer the right to terminate you because of race or disability, for example, even if it does not explicitly say this.

The ideal way to avoid this situation is to have a severance clause. If you are terminated, you will get an agreed-upon amount of compensation as severance pay. Severance pay was once strictly the domain of high-level executives. However, it is becoming more common for nonexecutive employees to receive these payments, so ask for such a clause in your contract.

To successfully negotiate a severance package, you must anticipate the various ways you may depart the company. Let's take an example from the employment agreement of Robert Russo, who was hired as VA-Linux's senior vice president and general manager of worldwide field operations:

(A) Involuntary Resignation. If you are Involuntarily Terminated from the Company within the first year of employment, you will receive six months' base compensation inclusive of all benefits and six months' vesting of stock. If you are Involuntarily Terminated after the first year of employment, you will receive three months' base compensation and three months' continued vesting. In the event a new CEO is named during the first twelve months of employment, the Employee will accelerate 25 percent of the initial stock grant if employee is terminated for any reason within the longer of (a) six months of the new CEO being named or (b) twelve months from employee start date.

(B) Change of Control Termination. Accelerated vesting of initial option grant on Change of Control and Involuntary Termination: You will receive twelve additional months of accelerated vesting of your initial option grant upon (a) a Change of Control and (b) Involuntary Termination within six months of Change of Control.

(C) Voluntary Resignation: Termination for Cause. If the Employee voluntarily resigns from the Company (other than a resignation that is an Involuntary Termination), or if the Company terminates the Employee's employment for Cause, then the Employee shall not be entitled to receive severance or other benefits except for those, if any, as may then be established under the Company's then-existing severance and benefits plans and policies at the time of such resignation or termination.

As you can see, a severance package will usually include acceleration of the vesting of your options and perhaps even cash payments.

Here's how accelerated vesting works: Suppose you have options to buy 5,000 shares of XYZ. The vesting period is five years. XYZ fires you within six months. You get 50 percent of the shares that would have vested for year one, which is 500 shares.

Make sure that "cause" and "change of control" are clearly defined. If not, litigation could be very costly in the event of a dispute. Depending on your company's policy, cause may include such things as:

➤ revealing the company's trade secrets
➤ an act of fraud or embezzlement
➤ an act of dishonesty or misconduct that impairs a business's goodwill or reputation
➤ a conviction for a felony involving an act of dishonesty, moral turpitude, deceit, or fraud
➤ material failure to perform lawful duties to the company

As for change of control, this refers to the ownership of your company changing hands. In this case, your job could be in jeopardy. Again, the precise definition of a change of control will depend on your company's policy. Here's what the concept means at Ariba, a business-to-business software company:

➤ merger or consolidation after which existing Ariba shareholders own less than 50 percent of the surviving corporation
➤ sale of all or substantially all of the assets of Ariba
➤ a proxy fight that results in the removal of more than one-third of the directors over a two-year period
➤ acquisition of 50 percent or more of the outstanding stock by a person not related to Ariba

Qualcomm, a leading-edge communications company, is a good example of the change of control clause. In March 1999 the company announced it would sell its network equipment manufacturing division to LM Ericsson. The division had 1,070 employees. Unfortunately, Qualcomm advised these employees that all unvested options would be terminated.

The Qualcomm option plan did have a change of control clause. If there had been a change of control of a majority of the company stock without board approval, then all options vesting would accelerate 100 percent. However, the clause did not mention a change of control of a division. In other words, the clause did not apply to the division's 1,070 employees. These employees have filed suit against Qualcomm, but the case is still pending.

If you work for a division of a company (versus working for corporate headquarters), it is a good idea to negotiate for a change of control clause that vests your options 100 percent if the division is sold. If you don't, you may lose a substantial amount of gains.

It is also possible for a company to spin off one of its divisions. In 1996, AT&T spun off its Lucent Technologies division by selling shares of the company to the public. As a result, Lucent became an independent public company.

Suppose you are an employee of a division that is spun off. In this case, the parent company will terminate your position and then the division will hire you. As a result, you will lose the options in the parent company, but the spun-off division will issue you new options. Typically, the terms and value of the new options will be equivalent to the options you had with the parent. Look at your options contract carefully to make sure. If there is no clause specifically outlining that your new options are equivalent to the old ones, the company might make the new option package less advantageous than your original package.

On the other hand, you could also reap some significant advantages as an employee of the spun-off company. As with any IPO, you could do quite well if the new company succeeds in the marketplace.

Finally, check your company's definition of a "leave of absence." The IRS sometimes treats a "leave of absence" as a termination. To get qualified tax treatment for ISOs (that is, for the profit you earn to be treated as a capital gain), you must be an employee from the time of the grant until the exercise. What is an employee? Basically, in order to be considered an employee, you must be subject to withholding taxes under federal law.

There are some exceptions. If the leave is the result of sickness, military engagement (active duty), or other bona fide reason and does not exceed ninety days, you still receive favorable tax treatment. If the leave is longer, then you may still get special tax treatment if your right to employment is guaranteed by statute or by contract with your employer. For example, some plans will provide that an employee may exercise options up to a year after termination of employment, as long as the employee is "permanently and totally disabled."

Notice

A NOTICE CLAUSE CAN HELP ENSURE that you receive important information on your stock options or that your company receives important information from you, such as instructions for exercising the options. The key to a notice clause is making sure that the notice has actually been sent to and acknowledged by the other party. For example, the Avanex notice clause below provides for either delivering the notice by hand or through certified mail. If you have such a clause in your contract, you also should indicate any change of address.

> Notices. All notices, requests, demands, and other communications called for hereunder shall be in writing and shall be deemed given if delivered personally or three (3) days after being mailed by registered or certified mail, return receipt requested, prepaid and addressed to the parties or their successors in interest at the following addresses, or at such other addresses as the parties may designate by written notice in the manner aforesaid.

> If to the Company: Avanex Corporation, 42501 Albrae Avenue, Fremont, CA 94538

> If to Executive: William Lanfri, at the last residential address known by the Company.

Assignment

AN ASSIGNMENT CLAUSE INDICATES to whom you can transfer the rights and benefits of your contract. In the example shown, the executive cannot assign the contract to anyone else. After all, the company is entering an agreement with him to perform duties. The contract is meant specifically for him. However, if he dies, any rights or benefits of the contract—such as severance or in-the-money stock options—can be assigned through a will or trust.

Finally, if Avanex merges with or is bought by another company, the employment contract must be assigned to the purchaser. It will be as if the purchaser had entered the agreement with the CEO. In other words, the CEO will retain the same protections as stated in his employment contract. Here's the assignment clause:

Assignment. This Agreement shall be binding upon and inure to the benefit of (a) the heirs, executors, and legal representatives of Executive upon Executive's death and (b) any successor of the Company. Any such successor of the Company shall be deemed substituted for the Company under the terms of this Agreement for all purposes. As used herein, "successor" shall include any person, firm, corporation, or other business entity which at any time, whether by purchase, merger, or otherwise, directly or indirectly acquires all or substantially all of the assets or business of the Company. None of the rights of Executive to receive any form of compensation payable pursuant to this Agreement shall be assignable or transferable except through a testamentary disposition or by the laws of descent and distribution upon the death of Executive following termination without cause. Any attempted assignment, transfer, conveyance, or other disposition (other than as aforesaid) of any interest in the rights of Executive to receive any form of compensation hereunder shall be null and void.

Entire Agreement

IN ESSENCE, THIS CLAUSE INDICATES that the contract is final and supersedes other agreements. Suppose you had an oral agreement that your company would offer an option of 10,000 shares if the company went public. According to this clause, this deal would not be valid. In fact, the clause even invalidates written agreements. Thus, before signing your contract, make sure it includes everything you want. Don't simply take your employer's word for it.

This is the entire agreement clause from the Avanex employment agreement:

Entire Agreement. This Agreement, the Company's 1998 Stock Plan, the Stock Option Agreement, and the Proprietary Information Agreement represent the entire agreement and understanding between the Company and Executive concerning Executive's employment relationship with the Company, which supersedes and replaces any and all prior agreements and understandings concerning Executive's employment relationship with the Company.

Modification

MANY CONTRACTS WILL SPECIFY that the agreement can be changed only in writing and only if the document is signed by both the employee and the company. Therefore, if you negotiate for another stock option grant, for example, you and the company must document this in writing.

Severability

SEVERABILITY IS A STANDARD CLAUSE. This means that if a certain clause is invalidated—perhaps in a foreign country where the government may rule a certain type of stock option is illegal—the rest of the provisions are still enforceable. Here is the typical wording:

> Severability. In the event that any provision hereof becomes or is declared by a court of competent jurisdiction to be illegal, unenforceable, or void, this Agreement shall continue in full force and effect without said provision.

Dispute Resolution

EVEN A STRONG CONTRACT is still not completely safe from litigation. But well-constructed contract language can indicate how to settle the dispute. One approach is the traditional court system. Unfortunately, this can be very expensive and time-consuming, although a jury is typically more sympathetic to an employee.

Another approach is arbitration, which allows for the resolution of a dispute based on the decision of a neutral third party, which can be either one person (an arbitrator) or a panel of arbitrators. Arbitration has many advantages. It tends to be cheaper and faster than litigation. But once a decision is made, it's final. There is no appeal. Also, the arbitrator may not necessarily be familiar with the intricacies of the laws for employee stock options.

As an example, take a look at a typical dispute resolution clause:

In the event of any dispute or claim relating to or arising out of our employment relationship, you and the Company agree that all such disputes shall be fully and finally resolved by binding arbitration conducted by the American Arbitration Association in Alameda County, California. However, we agree that this arbitration provision shall not apply to any disputes or claims relating to or arising out of the misuse or misappropriation of the Company's trade secrets or proprietary information.

Be careful to note where the dispute will be resolved. In many cases, the clause will indicate your state of residence. However, if your employer is based in a different state, then any disputes that arise may have to be resolved in the employer's state. You would then have to hire out-of-state counsel, which can be very costly. Therefore, try to make sure the forum clause has your state of residence.

Along similar lines, "governing law" clauses indicate which state laws "govern" for the purposes of settling any disputes. In most cases, it is the law stated in the forum clause.

Floors

THERE ARE NO GUARANTEES on the future price of a stock. You might work for a company for one year, only to see the stock price flounder. Although it is not easy, some people are able to negotiate floors to their stock option grants. Then if the stock does fall, they still receive a minimum amount of compensation.

Webvan is a case in point. This online grocery store hired Arvind Relan as the senior vice president of technology. If he is terminated, then he gets either his options vested in full or a sum of $3 million. The $3 million is the floor on the contract.

Consulting Agreements

AS COMPANIES GROW, THEY OFTEN replace the original senior executives because they begin to need more experienced operational executives who understand the complex issues of corporate organizations. The original executives may be retained as consultants. Of course, the transition to such an arrangement can be set out ahead of time in your employment agreement. If it is, you can specify how many hours you will work, the types of duties you will have, and the details of cash and stock compensation.

Example: Egreetings Network is a leading provider of online greeting cards. Gordon Tucker replaced Frederick Campbell as CEO of the company. Tucker received a salary of $225,000 and options to buy 2.2 million shares at $2.10 each when the company was private. Campbell, however, was retained as the company's chief financial officer until a new one was hired in July 1999. He also agreed to provide consulting services until August 2000, for a salary of $125,000.

Anthony Levitan was also replaced as president and chief concept officer. He agreed to provide consulting services until August 2001, for which he would receive a total of $214,500. He also received two severance payments of $87,000.

Confidentiality and Noncompetition

AN EMPLOYER DOES NOT WANT you to disclose any material information to others that may damage the company. So in most cases companies will require you to sign an option agreement with a confidentiality and noncompetition clause. A noncompetition clause specifies that you cannot work for a competitor for a certain period of time after termination. If you breach these clauses, the company may try to revoke your options. So be careful what you say and where you work next.

There are various types of forfeiture provisions regarding noncompetition and confidentiality:

➤ **Claw-backs (also known as callbacks).** Any gains that you derived from exercising your stock options must be returned to your employer when you leave to work for a competitor or when you violate the company's confidentiality policies. Also, you forfeit all your vested and unvested options.

➤ **Bad-boy provision.** You forfeit all vested and unvested options when you leave your employer or violate the company's confidentiality policies.

Although there are only a few court cases on the enforceability of such provisions, so far the courts have sided with employers.

Basically, the courts want to know whether the provisions are reasonable—whether there are time limits. Courts typically have viewed stock options as not part of an employee's basic compensation, like wages and pensions, so they do not get the same protections. What's more, courts have observed that the forfeiture provisions do not actually prevent an employee from working for other companies.

IBM has claw-back provisions in its stock option agreements (the employee forfeits all gains for the last six months of employment). And the company has aggressively enforced the provisions by litigating against former employees.

In the case IBM v. Martson, the federal district court held that IBM's contract provisions were enforceable. This was so even though the employee was based in California, where noncompetition clauses are tough to enforce. The court decided to apply the laws of New York, where IBM is based.

According to the court, the IBM contract was not a true noncompete. After all, the employee was not prevented from working for a competitor. Rather, there was only a disincentive to do so.

Company-Paid Financial Planning

WHEN WORKING FOR A FAST-PACED company, you may be too busy to handle your own financial matters. However, poor planning—or no planning—can cost you a great deal of money.

Some people will negotiate for an employer-paid financial planner. For complex financial situations, a planner may charge more than $20,000 per year.

Actually, a company may like the idea of providing this benefit, because theoretically the employee will spend more time focusing on his or her job. Also, some companies feel more comfortable with this type of benefit than with more peripheral ones, such as a company car or country club membership.

What's more, company-paid financial planning is not just for elite executives. More companies are starting to provide such benefits to middle managers.

Stock Split

A STOCK SPLIT OCCURS when a company issues more shares of stock to existing shareholders. The split is expressed as a ratio. In a 2-for-1 stock split, each shareholder gets two shares for each one owned. In a 3-for-1, each shareholder gets three shares for each one owned, and so on.

Since a stock split has no economic impact on the company, the price of the company's shares will decline accordingly. Suppose XYZ declares a 2-for-1 stock split and the fair market value of the stock is $40. Immediately after the split, the stock should be worth about $20.

As for your stock options, make sure that they are adjusted for any stock splits. Here is an example of some typical wording, from the employment agreement of Stephen Dukker, the CEO of eMachines, a low-cost PC marketer:

> Stock Splits, Dividends, and Combinations. In the event that the Company shall at any time subdivide the outstanding shares of Common Stock or shall issue a stock dividend on its outstanding shares of Common Stock, the number of Shares issuable upon exercise of this Option immediately prior to such subdivision or to the issuance of such stock dividend shall be proportionately increased, and the Exercise Price shall be proportionately decreased, and in the event that the Company shall at any time combine the outstanding shares of Common Stock, the number of Shares issuable upon exercise of this Option immediately prior to such combination shall be proportionately decreased, and the Exercise Price shall be proportionately increased, effective at the close of business on the date of such subdivision, stock dividend, or combination, as the case may be.

If you do not build in this provision when you are negotiating your option contract, the value of your options could be reduced substantially in the event of a stock split.

Computer Associates, a billion-dollar software giant, is a stark example of this. In 1995, the company's shareholders approved large stock option grants to three executives (up to 6 million shares). If the stock reached $180 per share for sixty days during a twelve-month period, then all of the stock would be granted. However, the legal document was poorly written and did not adequately account for splits in the company stock, of which there have been several since 1995. Despite this, the board of directors granted the shares adjusted for the splits.

Shareholders of Computer Associates litigated the case. And the Delaware Chancery Court ruled in favor of the shareholders. In all, the executives had to return 9.5 million shares. That amounted to about $558 million—making it the largest stock giveback in corporate history.

Attorneys' Fees

THIS CLAUSE IS FROM the employment agreement of Martha Stewart, CEO of Martha Stewart Living Omnimedia:

> Legal Fees and Expenses. If any contest or dispute shall arise between the Company and the Executive regarding any provision of this Agreement, the Company shall reimburse the Executive for all legal fees and expenses reasonably incurred by the Executive in connection with such contest or dispute, but only if the Executive prevails to a substantial extent with respect to the Executive's claims brought and pursued in connection with such contest or dispute. Such reimbursement shall be made as soon as practicable following the resolution of such contest or dispute (whether or not appealed) to the extent the Company receives reasonable written evidence of such fees and expenses.

In the above clause, if Martha Stewart successfully sued her company, she would be reimbursed the "reasonable" amount of her attorneys' fees. The court determines what is "reasonable." Yet if she lost the case, she would not be required to pay the company's fees.

Of course, such litigation can be extremely expensive. Make sure you are not responsible for your company's legal fees, although not all states uphold such provisions.

On another issue, it may be costly to negotiate your employment agreement with your prospective employer. In this case, you can insert a contract clause that requires the employer to pay all reasonable professional fees in connection with the employment agreement.

This is not common simply because most people do not think about it, but since the legal fees will probably be no more than $5,000 for most people, you might be able to get your employer to grant this concession. In a way, it could almost be part of the signing bonus.

Lockup Provisions

A LOCKUP PROVISION PERTAINS to an IPO and is a contract between the company that is going public and its underwriter. Basically, executive officers, directors, major shareholders, and usually most option holders are prohibited from selling their stock within 180 days of the IPO. Sometimes a company with lots of clout can shorten the lockup period. This was the case with eBay and Juniper Networks, both of which had lockups of only four months.

The reason for the lockup is that the underwriter does not want to see undue selling pressure on the stock when the company does its IPO. After all, if an IPO soars 100 percent or more on the first day, it would be very tempting to unload shares—especially since many of these options were issued at a low price and could now be worth millions.

You can find the lockup provision in the company's prospectus. What's more, your company will probably require you to sign a document that puts you under the obligations of the lockup provision when you get an option grant. In most cases, there is no way to negotiate the lockup.

Here's a sample lockup provision from the employee stock option plan of Red Hat, a leading Internet software company:

> Lockup Agreement. The Optionee agrees that in connection with any underwritten public offering of Common Stock, upon the request of the Company or the principal underwriter managing such public offering, the Option Shares may not be sold, offered for sale, or otherwise disposed of without the prior written consent of the Company or such underwriter, as the case may be, for at least 180 days after the execution of an underwriting agreement in connection with such offering, or such longer period of time as the Board of Directors may determine if all of the Company's directors and executive officers agree to be similarly bound. The obligations under this Section 17

shall remain effective for all underwritten public offerings with respect to which the Company has filed a registration statement on or before the date two (2) years after the closing of the Company's initial public offering; provided, however, that this Section 17 shall cease to apply to any Option Shares sold to the public pursuant to an effective registration statement or an exemption from the registration requirements of the Securities Act in a transaction that complied with the terms of this Agreement.

As you can imagine, many option holders pay close attention to their calendars, waiting for the lockup period to expire so they can cash in on their stock options. But bear in mind that this is not always a good idea. After all, many other option holders probably will do the same, since the stock typically declines. A stark example of this was Healtheon, a high-flying health-care Internet company. On August 10, 1999, the day the company's lockup period expired, the stock plunged 21 percent.

But keep in mind that the lockup sell-off is usually temporary, if it occurs at all. Usually the officers and founders own a large chunk of the stock, and since they probably believe strongly in the future of the company, they may sell little or none of their holdings.

Finally, remember that family members are also covered under the lockup period. A famous case involved the ABC News health correspondent Nancy Snyderman. She was a director of the online health portal drkoop.com. Her husband made a stock trade in drkoop.com within a month of the IPO, which was a violation of the lockup provision. He had to return about $53,000.

Repricing

REPRICING MEANS THAT THE MANAGEMENT of a company lowers the exercise price on existing options—usually because the stock price has collapsed. In this case, employees have options that are considered "under water."

Suppose you were granted stock options when the price of the company's stock was $55 per share. Then the company announces it must restate its earnings for the past two years. The stock goes into a free fall, landing at $10 per share. Thus, for your options to have any value, the stock price will need to increase more than fivefold.

Under such circumstances employees may be inclined to leave, because they no longer have much equity incentive. Repricing helps to solve this problem, and it has been done at such companies as Netscape and Apple Computers.

There are two ways of handling a repricing:

Option amendment. This is the most common (and the easiest for a corporation). Basically, current stock option agreements are amended with a new exercise price. The option holder may also have to make certain types of concessions, such as restarting the vesting period, undergoing a blackout period (that is, you cannot exercise the options for a certain period of time), or even giving back some shares from the existing grant.

Option exchange. In this scenario, a corporation replaces the old agreement with a completely new one. You will hand in your old contract, and it will no longer be valid. In the transaction, you should receive a contract that specifies the terms of the new arrangement, as well as a new option contract. If not, request both documents.

You are not required to accept the repricing (you typically have thirty days to make the decision). For example, you might be very optimistic about the company and feel its stock will rebound sooner. What's more, you already have 30 percent of the shares vested and thus would be able to exercise the options sooner. This may be favorable if you do not plan to stay with the company much longer.

Repricing sounds wonderful, but it is not very common. Under current accounting rules, repricing will usually result in significant charges against earnings. Also, institutional shareholders do not like repricings and may not approve them.

For tax purposes, the IRS considers a repricing a modification to an ISO and therefore treats it as a new grant. The holding period for the options will be restarted. Therefore, to get favorable tax treatment, you need to hold on to the stock for two years after the repricing and one year from the date of exercise of the new option contract.

When a company reprices its options' exercise price, the fair market value of the shares covered by the option agreement—those that are exercisable for the calendar year—may exceed $100,000. If so, the excess amount would not be given favorable tax treatment and would instead be considered a nonqual.

Key Issues to Consider

➤ How is your employment classified? Are you an employee-at-will? If so, your employer can revoke your options for any reason. Find out if you can insert any clauses to protect your options—such as a clause for a severance package or special vesting (having a portion of your options vest every quarter instead of once a year).

➤ Most employment and option agreements have clauses that prevent you from disclosing confidential information, so be wary. If you violate such clauses, you will forfeit your options—perhaps even those that have already vested and been exercised.

➤ Another common clause is noncompetition. That is, your employer does not want you working for a competitor. Violating the clause can have serious consequences, such as losing your options—even if you have already vested or exercised them.

➤ How will any disputes over your option contract be settled? Will it be through arbitration or the court system? For the most part, arbitration is cheaper and faster. Also, in what state will any disputes be decided? Keep in mind that if it is not in your home state, it can be an onerous process for you.

➤ Occasionally a company will split its stock. Make sure your contract provides that the company will adjust the quantity of your shares accordingly.

➤ If you decide to litigate your option contract, will you be liable for the legal fees if you lose? Try to eliminate this clause.

➤ If your company is bought by or merged with another company, you might lose your unvested options if you are laid off. One protection is accelerated vesting, in which part or all of your options vest when there is a "change of control," although this can be tough to negotiate.

Chapter Seven

Options in Private Companies

L IVING.COM WAS ON the Internet fast track. A leader in selling
furniture over the Web, the company was able to attract big
investors, such as Benchmark Capital, Amazon.com, and even
Starbucks Coffee Company. Living.com had a top-notch site and
major suppliers and partners.

It seemed as if the company were destined for a huge IPO.
Unfortunately, consumers were not willing to buy furniture over the
Web, and the company quickly ran out of money. By August 2000,
Living.com was no longer living: the company filed for bankruptcy
and laid off 275 employees. Of course, the options of every single
employee became worthless.

This story is not uncommon. Small private companies have a high
failure rate. In fact, about 90 percent of them fail within the first five
years for reasons ranging from bad management to competition, poor
timing, insufficient capital, and incompetent execution.

Therefore, before accepting a job at a small company (most of
which are also private companies), be realistic. Don't think it will be
a smooth ride. Most likely, it will be a roller coaster. But if things work
out, the upside can be huge.

Liquidity

SUPPOSE A HOT HIGH-TECH FIRM hires you. The company grants you 4,000 options at 10¢ per share. The options vest over a four-year period. A year passes, and 1,000 of your shares vest, so you decide to exercise the options. The problem: to whom do you sell the shares? After all, there is no public market for the shares, because the company is private. True, the company said it was planning to go public and list on Nasdaq, but so far this has not happened. What can you do?

Basically, the big problem with private stock options and shares is liquidity. A private company may have its own system to allow employees to sell their shares, although this is extremely rare. Perhaps the best example of this is Science Applications International Corporation (SAIC), which is a scientific consulting firm with about 25,000 employees and $3.4 billion in revenues.

SAIC has created an internal stock exchange called Bull for employees. In fact, the system has been registered with the Securities and Exchange Commission. The board of directors of SAIC sets the stock price four times each year. The price is based on a complex formula that accounts for revenues, profits, and outstanding shares. An outside valuation firm, Houlihan, Lokey, Howard & Zukin, computes the formula.

One strategy for private-share liquidity is a "private sale." As long as you have no restrictions on your shares, you can sell them to a third party. Unfortunately, it can be extremely difficult to find people willing to buy the shares, because a buyer would be assuming the same liquidity risks that you have. Of course, there is also the huge risk that the private company will fail. Thus, when you do a private sale, the price is typically at a steep discount to its current value, as established by the company's appraiser.

A good way to find private buyers is to contact a major brokerage firm. Some brokers specialize in this marketplace. They have clients who have the capital and are willing to undertake the risks of buying private stock. All the major wire houses, such as Merrill Lynch and J. P. Morgan, have such brokers.

An IPO is another way of getting liquidity for your shares. However, IPOs are also rare. In 1999, about 600 companies went public, out of 16 million businesses in the United States. Plus, IPOs can encounter many problems, as the first half of 2000 so clearly demonstrated. When the Nasdaq fell more than 30 percent, the IPO market plunged. In the second quarter, seventy-six companies withdrew their IPOs, and thirty-eight companies postponed them. Even well-established companies had trouble.

The more common scenario for private companies is a merger or acquisition. Let's take a look.

Mergers and Acquisitions (M&As)

LET'S SAY THAT ABC WANTS TO BUY XYZ. It can use several different approaches.

Cash. ABC can buy XYZ for cash. Example: ABC values XYZ at $10 per share, with 1 million shares outstanding. The price for the acquisition is $10 million.

Stock. ABC can exchange a portion of its shares for all of the shares of XYZ. Example: ABC's share price is $20 per share. ABC will compute the exchange ratio, which is the stock price for the acquisition of XYZ divided by the stock price of ABC. This is equal to 50¢ ($10 divided by $20). So for every share of XYZ you own, you get half a share of ABC.

Stock and cash. ABC can exchange a portion of its shares and cash for all the shares of XYZ.

Suppose you work for XYZ and have options to buy 10,000 shares at 1¢ per share. At the time of the acquisition, you have 2,000 shares that have vested. Now, in some cases, ABC will convert these options into its own shares. Since there is a 0.5 exchange ratio for the acquisition, you will have options on 4,000 shares of ABC. Note: The acquisition may require option holders of XYZ to exercise all vested options. If they do not, the options will be terminated.

If you have unvested options, these will probably be terminated when the acquisition takes place. Thus, it is important to negotiate ahead of time for 100 percent vesting of your stock options when a merger or acquisition occurs (in legal terms, this is called a "change of control" and is discussed further in Chapter 6). This is known as accelerated vesting.

Researching Private Companies

EVALUATING A PRIVATE COMPANY is not easy. First of all, private companies are not required to report their financial data, so it becomes much more difficult to separate fact from fiction. In fact, when you talk to the management of a private company, you will usually hear lots of optimism, such as "We plan to go public in six months," "Business is booming," and "We will land some major contracts." Many entrepreneurs who lead private companies are very convincing. Don't let this cloud your judgment. You need to be objective and find out as much as possible to make a smart decision.

Even though private companies do not file with the SEC, you can still get lots of useful information on the company. First, go to the company's Web site and look for the section usually called "About Us." Read the press releases. There is typically a section called "In the News," which has links to recent stories written about the company.

Visit competitors' sites. They also have lots of information. In fact, you may realize that working for the competitor is a better idea. Finally, check out the following general Web resources:

➤ **Hoover's Online** (www.hoovers.com). The site has a comprehensive database of private U.S. companies. A Hoover's private company profile will show officers, competition, market position, history, financial data, and products and services. A personal membership is $14.95 per month.

➤ **Dun & Bradstreet** (www.dnb.com). The company is a leader in providing background information on private companies. You can order a Business Background Report for $23 per company.

In addition to these Web resources, you can also take the more traditional route and research the company in the business section of your local library, obtaining information from business directories, magazine articles, newspapers, and other publications. Finally, ask the company for as much information as you can get. If management is reluctant to provide you with information, it may have something to hide.

What to Look For

BASICALLY, STOCK OPTIONS are a bet on the future of the company. So when selecting a company to work for, treat it as if you were making an investment.

Here are factors to consider:

➤ **Management.** Has company management been successful with other ventures? Have individual senior managers been able to raise venture capital and take companies public? Have they sold companies? You might find the résumés of key senior managers on the company's Web site. If not, request copies from the company.

➤ **Market potential.** Market niches do not make companies IPO candidates or buyout candidates. Rather, a company must be leading a charge in a potentially massive market. eBay is a great example. The company developed a concept called person-to-person auctions; that is, people could put up their products on eBay's Web site for others to bid on, and eBay would get a fee. Until eBay, this industry had an outlet mostly through flea markets and garage sales, and it was rather inefficient. Yet the market for flea markets and garage sales is about $50 billion per year, so it was clearly there to be tapped. Currently, eBay is the leader in the online person-to-person auction industry and has a market value of $7 billion.

➤ **Barriers to entry.** One of the common ways of protecting a market is with a patent. This is routinely done in the pharmaceutical industry. The government allows up to twenty years of patent protection for new drugs. After this, generic-drug companies can offer their own products.

Many high-tech companies now are also seeking patent protection. Priceline.com patented its unique online bid-auction system. The protection of a patent has allowed the company to enter a myriad of markets, such as airline tickets, cars, and even gasoline. Priceline.com has a market value of $4.5 billion, and sales were $482 million in 1999.

But patent protection is no guarantee of success, as Priceline's recent decision to eliminate its gasoline and grocery lines demonstrates. A company might have a patent on a product for which there is little demand. Some patents are weak and may be reverse-engineered. A patent must be filed with the Patent and Trademark Office, and all of its materials are available to the public. Copycat versions that dilute the company's competitive edge are a real danger.

➤ **Standards.** Some companies have been able to differentiate themselves in the marketplace by creating industry standards. For example, Microsoft has built its empire by creating uniform, integrated software systems. It created Windows standards, Internet standards, and networking standards. Recently, Palm Computing has been able to create a standard operating system for handheld devices. Investors have rewarded the company with a market value of $14 billion. If you're evaluating a private company whose product could potentially become an industry standard, you just might be in luck.

➤ **Venture capital.** A venture capital (VC) firm raises money from institutions and wealthy individuals and then invests the money in private companies with very strong prospects. The top venture capital firms have partners with a keen understanding of mergers and acquisitions and IPOs. They also help a company find executive talent, build the operational infrastructure, develop strategic partners and customers, and position the product. In a way, VC firms can act as management consultants. The top firms include Kleiner Perkins Caulfield & Beyers (www.kpcb.com), Sequoia Capital (www.sequoiacap.com), Benchmark Capital (www.benchmark.com), and Softbank Venture Capital (www.sbvc.com).

➤ **Strategic partners.** Critical to jump-starting the growth of a company is signing up key strategic partners, who are usually investors. These include the big guys, such as Microsoft, Intel, Cisco, and IBM. These companies can provide technology and distribution capabilities.

➤ **First mover.** Being the first on the block with a new product or service can be critical. While it does not guarantee long-term success, it certainly helps. After all, it does not take long for a company to dominate its industry, as Yahoo!, Amazon.com, and eBay have demonstrated. Look how hard it has been for barnesandnoble.com to catch up with Amazon.com: at last count, barnesandnoble.com had sales of $297 million; Amazon.com had sales of $2.4 *billion*.

Taxes

PRIVATE COMPANIES HAVE DIFFERENT types of structures, but whether your employer is a corporation, partnership, limited liability company, or S-corporation, the tax consequences for you do not change. They are the same as those discussed in the chapters about ISOs and nonqualified stock options.

Restrictions

WHEN A PRIVATE COMPANY ISSUES stock options, it must abide by complex securities regulations. If the company violates the regulations, then it may be required to file with the Securities and Exchange Commission, which is expensive and time-consuming.

If you exercise your stock options and get shares of a private company, you typically will need to sign an investment letter. In the document, you will agree to the following:

➢ You are aware of the company's business affairs and can make an informed decision about the purchase of the stock.

➢ You are purchasing the stock for your own account and not for the purpose of reselling it, which would be considered a "distribution" under securities regulations. That is, before you sell stock (you may be allowed to do so if the restrictions have lapsed), you must indicate what the purpose is so that the company does not violate securities regulations.

➢ You understand that the shares have not been registered with the Securities and Exchange Commission. This is printed on your stock certificates and is called a legend. You cannot sell the stock until the legend is removed (when the stock is registered, for example) or an exemption to the rule is obtained. An example of an exemption is Rule 701 (discussed in Chapter 5).

➢ You are familiar with Rule 144 (this is also discussed in Chapter 5).

What's more, a company will often impose a variety of restrictions on your shares, mainly because it wants to control who receives its shares. Obviously, the company does not want you to sell shares to a competitor. These restrictions may include the following:

➢ You must allow the founders to vote your shares for such important issues as new board members, an IPO, or a merger.

➤ You agree to a "right of first refusal." This means you give the right to the company to buy your shares at the price and terms you would set in selling to a third party.

➤ You agree to a "repurchase right." This gives the company the right to buy back your stock—even if you do not want to sell it. The price is either the fair market value, the book value (which is the net worth of the company), or the original purchase price. In terms of negotiating, try to negotiate the price as the fair market value; this is the most advantageous to you.

Start-up Company Culture

THERE ARE MANY ADVANTAGES to working for a major public company. Your role is fairly defined. The company is very unlikely to go bankrupt. If you have stock options, they are likely to increase in value over time.

But of course, there are many stresses. The bureaucracy can be maddening. The environment might not be entrepreneurial. And the upside for your stock options might not be as good as it would be with a pre-IPO company.

In light of all this, it is not surprising that employees have been leaving large companies to work for private start-up companies. The work environment at a private company can be fast-paced and invigorating. Your efforts can have a huge impact on the firm.

But again, you need to be careful and consider the complete picture. Before you sign on with a small company, you should be willing to accept these possibilities:

Fewer benefits. Many smaller private companies do not have traditional benefits, such as medical insurance and 401(k)s. You may need to pay for your own benefits.

Multitasking. To work for a small start-up company, you need to juggle various projects at the same time. That makes it crucial to learn strong time-management skills.

Long hours. Expect to work many hours. Typically, you will not have a well-defined, nine-to-five job. On the contrary, the pace will be frenetic at best.

Loose job titles. Titles often are not important in small companies.

Although this makes for a less clearly defined organizational structure, it does allow you to do things that go beyond your job title and to develop your professional skills. A start-up company, where there are never enough people to handle everything, is a perfect opportunity to get exposure to areas you might never learn about in a larger company. Don't limit yourself to your job description.

Key Issues to Consider

➤ Working for a private company has many risks. In other words, the chances of your options being worthless are quite high.

➤ For the most part, you have little or no liquidity for your options with a private company. Liquidity happens usually through a buyout or an IPO. And keep in mind that an IPO is quite rare.

➤ When deciding to work for a private company, treat it as if you were buying the company's stock. Does the company have barriers to entry? Is the market large? Is the management strong?

➤ A private company typically will have a variety of restrictions on its option plan. For example, the company may have the right to repurchase your stock, or you may be prevented from selling your stock to certain companies and individuals.

➤ The start-up culture can be a roller coaster. It is not for everyone.

Chapter Eight

International Stock Option Plans

W ITH THE GLOBALIZATION of the economy, the odds are increasing that you could work for a foreign company or that a foreign company could buy the one you are working for. If so, you might still be employed in the United States, but you will be subject to the employee stock option plan imposed by the foreign company. The rules vary greatly from country to country.

Or you may decide to work for an overseas division of your U.S.-based company. Before doing this, ask your employer which stock option plan applies—the U.S. plan or the local country's plan? The foreign plan may not be as advantageous as the U.S. plan. If so, make sure that you can continue under your current U.S. stock option plan during your stint abroad. This will depend on your employer's policies; there are no across-the-board regulations.

The most immediate problem for option holders arises if the foreign company does not list its stock on a U.S. exchange. That makes it difficult for the foreign company to issue options, since the grant is also subject to federal securities laws, which may be more stringent than those in the home country. Thankfully, in 1999 the Securities and Exchange Commission made it easier for foreign companies to issue options in the United States. Still, generally only major international companies provide stock option plans to U.S.-based employees. There are similarly onerous regulations that impede U.S. companies from offering options to employees based outside the United States.

Foreign Companies

THE UNITED STATES HAS well-developed laws on employee stock option plans, but things are less clear-cut in much of the rest of the world. Some countries, such as France, make it extremely difficult for companies to implement employee stock option plans. The capital gains tax rate on employee stock options there is 40 percent. If the option is exercised within five years of the grant, then ordinary income taxes also apply (the maximum is 56.8 percent). There is also a 2.4 percent general social contribution tax.

If you do not properly report the necessary taxes on your employee stock options, penalties can be severe. In Hong Kong, the penalty can be as much as 100 percent of the omitted income.

Some countries have unique option regulations. In the Netherlands, you owe taxes when your options vest. The taxes are based on the spread between the fair market value of the shares on the date of vesting and the option exercise price. This amount is then added to the "expectation value," an amount that attempts to estimate the probable increase in the value of the shares. The expectation ranges from 4 percent (for a sale within one year) to 35 percent (if the shares are sold after ten years).

Foreign tax structures for employee stock options can be extremely complex, and they require the help of a competent CPA. The rules and regulations for options may be very different, too, so having a strong attorney is crucial. You do not necessarily need a CPA or attorney based in the country in which you intend to work. However, make certain that your attorney and CPA have international experience. To help verify this, ask the CPA and attorney whether you can contact some of their clients. See Chapter 11 for more information on finding good advisers.

Let's examine the types of issues you should be aware of when dealing with foreign employee stock option plans. Before you accept any offers, ask the following questions:

Where is the company's stock listed? Is it listed in the United States? If it is listed in the United States, you might want to ensure that you have the right, spelled out in your option contract, to buy the company's stock here. After all, you probably have a broker in the United States, who probably also charges less in commissions. And the taxes might be lower here than in the foreign country.

What are the disclosure requirements for your stock markets? Do you follow the same requirements as the Securities and Exchange Commission in the United States? If not, then you might not be able to obtain adequate knowledge about the stock. This makes it difficult to know when to hold or sell your shares.

To have your company listed on your exchange, are you required to follow GAAP (generally accepted accounting principles)? GAAP is the body of standard rules for accounting of publicly traded U.S. companies, such as the requirement to publish quarterly reports and annual reports. GAAP also mandates reports for special situations, such as mergers and acquisitions. Many countries have their own particular accounting rules, which may not provide a clear picture of the company's circumstances. If this is the case, it may be worthwhile to buy a book that describes the country's accounting standards.

Does your country have any exchange controls? Some countries have strict rules to make it difficult for money to be transferred overseas. If your company has exchange controls, it may be tough, if not impossible, to transfer your money to the United States after you exercise your options.

Are stock options an entitlement in your country? If so, then stock options become included in your retirement, severance, and bonus compensation. This means that the company would have a difficult time revoking your stock options. But companies try to avoid having options classified as an entitlement, often by writing a clause in the options contract. For example, this can be done in Brazil, as long as the waiver is written in Portuguese.

What are the securities laws in the country? Does the country have special disclosure requirements for insiders? In other words, do you have to file statements with the national regulators? Are there holding periods, such as the short-swing rules here in the United States? Ask the company for any information it may have on the subject. If ever there was a case for asking the employer to include help from a financial adviser in the option package, this is it.

Are there any favorable tax moves I can make? For example, you can avoid the social charge in France if you get nonqualified stock options. In the Netherlands, you can avoid paying taxes when your options vest by getting "conditional stock options" (options that can be exercised only when management determines that certain conditions are met, such as holding periods).

Are taxes owed at the time options are granted? Some countries, such as Denmark, have this law, although overall it is rare. If you think the company does not have much upside, then you might want to decline the option grant to avoid paying the up-front taxes.

What does the terminology in my option contract mean? Make sure you understand all definitions in your contract, taking into account local idioms and terms. For example, in the United Kingdom, stock options are called "share options," and a stock option plan is called a "scheme."

What types of taxes are applied to stock options? Besides national taxes, there may also be state and local taxes on stock options. In Switzerland, for example, there are national taxes, which are mandated by the Swiss federal tax rules. Also, each canton, or state, within Switzerland has its own interpretation of these rules.

When weighing the potential value of options from a foreign country, you need to be aware of some other issues, too:

Cost of living. The cost of living can be high in some countries, such as Japan. Besides asking for higher wages, there are other strategies for dealing with these countries: increasing the moving allowance; asking for at least two months' rent money up front; asking to be paid at the beginning of each month; and requesting a cost-of-living allowance (that is, your salary increases in step with the rate of the country's inflation). To understand the country's cost of living, pay a visit in person. Also, talk with other expatriates who have worked there.

Living conditions. A great job offer with substantial options may mean working in a country that has problems with pollution, sanitation, crime, overcrowding, schools, and the health system. To encourage employees to work in these countries, companies may offer a "hardship" premium, in the form of a higher salary or better stock options, or in some cases, both.

Legal system. You need to be aware of foreign laws that could affect your living expenses. For example, China and Vietnam have strict laws on whether a foreign worker can drive a car. Often companies will provide their foreign workers with their own drivers. Also, some countries may not allow foreign workers to buy real estate. Instead, you may be required to rent an apartment.

Politics. In countries with harsh governments, capriciously enforced laws and strong constraints on freedom of speech can hurt foreign business and foreign employees. Your company could experience hard times or even bankruptcy. Another possibility is that your company might be nationalized, in which case you are likely to lose your stock options.

Currency risk. If you hold foreign stock as a result of a stock option exercise, you run the risk that the value of your investment in dollar terms may fall because of currency fluctuations, which can be substantial. It is not unheard of for currencies to swing 20 percent to 30 percent in a year relative to a major reference currency, such as the euro, dollar, or yen. For example, suppose your options are denominated in Italian lire because your company is based there. You exercise the options, but the currency falls by 20 percent in value, and then you sell the stock. When you convert your lire into U.S. dollars, the value of your holdings will have declined by 20 percent.

But if you work for a U.S. company that has a division in Italy, ask that your options be denominated in dollars. This safeguards you from any currency risk.

Accelerated Vesting

SUPPOSE THAT YOU AGREE to work for a company and get an option to buy 10,000 shares of its stock for $10 each. The vesting period is two years. After six months, the company is bought by a foreign company, which is based in a country that does not recognize employee stock options. As part of the merger, the employee option plan is terminated.

Although this sounds unlikely, it does happen. One protection against this is to have a clause in your option agreement requiring that all or a portion of your shares vest immediately whenever there is a "change of control" of the company, such as a merger or a buyout.

Advantages

IN ALERTING YOU TO THE RISKS of accepting options from foreign companies, I don't mean to imply that you should not accept these options—merely that you should be cautious and well-informed.

Actually, the upside of stock options from a foreign company can be tremendous. Here are a few advantages:

➤ **Getting in on the ground floor.** Many countries are poised for strong growth over the next few decades. They are undergoing deregulation and introducing expansive economic policies. Also, new technologies are making it easier for many nations to grow faster. There is the possibility that you may get a job with the next Yahoo! or eBay.

➤ **Shareholder changes.** Attitudes toward stock ownership are starting to change. Countries in Europe and Asia are seeing much more participation by individual investors in their stock exchanges. This should add impetus to stock values.

➤ **Career growth.** Having international experience is highly valuable. Companies understand that a global perspective is crucial. With international work experience, you increase your chances of moving up the corporate ladder at home.

➤ **Start-ups.** Many countries are encouraging and rewarding entrepreneurial efforts, which should further enhance growth. In fact, U.S. venture capital firms are starting to invest overseas.

A Smorgasbord of Option Plans

OFTEN, FOREIGN COMPANIES WILL LOOK to the United States as the model for drafting an employee stock option plan. A big reason is that these companies have operations in the United States, plus they want to issue their stock on a U.S. exchange. Here's a look at some stock option plans from around the globe:

Carrier1. Developer of a sophisticated Internet network throughout Europe, the company is based in Zurich, Switzerland. In 1999, the board of directors of Carrier1 approved a stock option plan. The maximum number of shares to be issued under the plan is 2.7 million. Moreover, the exercise price may not be lower than $2 per share. Options are ISOs and vest in equal installments over a five-year period.

Satyam Infoway. A leading portal site in India, the company went public in October 1999 at $18 per share. On its first day of trading, the stock hit $35.50.

The company's board of directors approved its stock option plan, called the Associates Stock Option Plan (ASOP), in March 1999. In all, 825,000 shares were reserved for the plan. Actually, the plan is quite complex. Satyam established a trust, known as the Satyam Infoway Associate Trust, which bought the 825,000 shares. When a grant is made, the trust issues options to the employee. The vesting and exercise price is indicated in the option.

Exercising the option is called conversion. Before this date, if the employee leaves or is terminated, the options revert back to the trust.

When the employee wants to convert shares, he or she must submit a letter to the trust, as well as payment for the shares. The shares received will be those listed on the Indian stock exchange. An employee can also convert these shares to those listed on Nasdaq.

El Sitio. This is an Internet service provider based in Buenos Aires, Argentina. The IPO took place in December 1999 at $16 per share. The stock closed at $33.31 on its first day of trading.

The company's 1999 stock option plans provide for 3.2 million shares to be issued. The plans cover both ISOs and nonquals. No one may receive more than 15 percent of the total options issuable under the plan. Employees may choose between two types of vesting arrangements. One approach is to vest 30 percent each year for the first two years and then 40 percent in the third year. Or employees can arrange to have all options vest in the third year.

Key Issues to Consider

➤ Other countries may have very different securities regulations from those of the United States. Make sure you understand the rules, because the consequences of violations can be severe.

➤ It may be difficult to liquidate your option gains from foreign companies. Some countries, for example, have exchange controls. Or the options may be based on a stock listed on a foreign exchange, which may not be very liquid.

➤ Every country has its own tax laws relating to stock options, and in some countries, options are taxed at the time of the grant. You need a professional who understands the nuances.

➤ Owning foreign securities carries many risks, such as currency fluctuations and political instability.

➤ Although working overseas can be a great experience and may also provide much financial upside, the living conditions may be lackluster.

C h a p t e r **9** *N i n e*

Other Types of Equity Plans

S TOCK OPTIONS ARE JUST ONE FORM of equity-based compensation. Your employer may also offer you other incentives, such as phantom stock, stock appreciation rights, direct stock purchase plans, and 401(k)s, and it's important to be able to distinguish among them. These plans may share characteristics of stock options, but they are definitely not stock options.

Still, other equity plans can complement your stock-option strategies nicely. For example, you might use the proceeds to exercise stock options or pay taxes on them. Consult with your financial advisers on the specifics of these incentives and how they may affect your stock-option strategy.

Section 423 Discount Purchase Plans

NAMED AFTER A SECTION in the IRS Code, a Section 423 discount purchase plan (also known as an employee stock purchase plan, or ESPP for short) allows most employees to participate, as long as the following rules apply:

➢ The employee does not own 5 percent or more of the company's stock.

➢ The employee works at least twenty hours per week.

➢ The employee works a minimum of five months per calendar year.

➢ The employee has been with the company for at least two years.

111

The employee may not buy more than $25,000 of the stock within each calendar year.

The transaction is usually done via payroll deductions. For example, suppose you work for a company that allows you to make purchases every quarter. In the most recent quarter, you bought 1,000 shares. What price do you get? Typically, it is 85 percent of the lower of the stock values at the beginning or end of the quarter. Let's say that the stock price was $20 at the beginning of the quarter and $25 at the end. The company allows you to make the purchase at 85 percent of the $20, the maximum discount allowed. Thus, your purchase price would be $17.

Even though you receive a discount, you do not owe taxes. Rather, you pay them when you sell your shares. However, the taxes on the 15 percent discount are treated as ordinary income, and the remaining appreciation is considered capital gains.

If your company does not meet the requirements of Section 423, it may offer an "open-market purchase plan." With this, you can buy stock—with no discounts—by using payroll deductions. What's the benefit? You do not have to pay any brokerage commissions.

Example of a Section 423 plan: Ashford.com (ASFD) is a leading online retailer of luxury goods. The company went public in September 1999 at $13 per share.

The board of directors approved the stock purchase plan in July 1999, and the compensation committee has the duty to oversee the plan. There were 950,000 shares reserved. Each offering period lasts twenty-four months. Two overlapping offering periods begin on May 1 and November 1 of each year. The purchases of the common stock occur on April 30 and October 31 of each year during an offering period. No employee can buy more than 950 shares on any purchase date, and employees can end their participation in the plan at any time. In the event of a change of control of Ashford.com, the stock purchase plan will end and shares will be bought with the payroll deductions accumulated to date by participating employees—that is, unless the plan is adopted by the succeeding corporation.

Employee Stock Ownership Plans (ESOPs)

AN ESOP IS REALLY A retirement plan whose chief asset is the stock of the company you work for. An ESOP includes most employees of a company. In most cases the company, not the employee, pays for the stock. Here's how it works: Your employer decides to establish an ESOP. It creates a trust, to which it will transfer shares that are periodically allocated to employees, usually based on pay levels and years of service. Like stock options, an employee's interest in the stock will vest over time—for example, 20 percent per year, although some companies may have immediate vesting.

To qualify, an employee usually must be full-time, be twenty-one years of age or older, and have worked for the company for at least one year (1,000 hours).

Employees do not have access to their ESOP assets until retirement, disability, or death. Thus, you are taking on lots of risk, as you are betting on only one investment: your company's stock. Also, you cannot use the ESOP funds to exercise employee stock options.

However, if you are fifty-five years old and have worked at your company for a minimum of ten years, you are allowed to diversify 25 percent of your ESOP account into other investments. By age sixty, you can diversify up to 50 percent.

401(k) Plans and Stock Ownership

A 401(K) IS A RETIREMENT PLAN that allows you to contribute pretax dollars and invest them in tax-deferred investment vehicles. In most cases, you can allocate your contributions into a variety of mutual funds, such as growth, international, biotech, and so on. Some companies allow you to buy their stock or match your contributions in company stock (these situations do not involve stock options).

If you already have a large amount of stock options, it may not necessarily be a good idea to use your 401(k) to buy stock in your company. You may be taking unnecessary risks by placing a large percentage of your net worth in one investment.

Over the years, you probably will build up some substantial assets in your 401(k), and it may be tempting to withdraw funds to exercise your stock options. But you should be aware that the IRS has strict rules on withdrawing funds. Unless there is a hardship (such as disability), a withdrawal before age fifty-nine-and-a-half will mean a 10 percent penalty, as well as full taxes on the amount withdrawn.

Another idea is to take a loan from a 401(k). Like any loan, you will pay interest on it, although the interest rates are much lower than credit card rates. Actually, you are paying yourself interest, since the interest payments go back into the 401(k) fund. But this is not as good as it sounds. The funds you use to pay the interest are after-tax funds. Therefore, when you retire, you will pay taxes on the interest amount.

There are other things to consider. For example, if you leave the company, whether voluntarily or not, you probably will need to repay the loan. If you cannot pay back the loan, then the loan amount will be considered a withdrawal, and you will be subject to the 10 percent penalty and income taxes.

Here's another scenario: You have 10,000 shares of XYZ in your 401(k). You also have an option for 5,000 shares of XYZ. You decide to exercise the option by using the shares from your 401(k). Unfortunately, you can't do that, because you do not hold title to the shares in the 401(k); rather, the plan trustee has title.

Finally, be aware of the consequences of nonquals on your 401(k). The limit for 401(k) contributions is the lesser of $10,500 or 15 percent of your W-2 income. Since the exercise of nonquals increases your W-2 income, this could make it possible for you to contribute more money to your 401(k). Example: You have a salary of $50,000 per year. You can make a contribution of $7,500 ($50,000 times 15 percent). But suppose you exercise $100,000 in nonquals. In this case, you would be able to contribute $10,500 to your 401(k). This is the maximum amount you can contribute, since 15 percent of $150,000 in total compensation would be more than $10,500.

Phantom Stock versus Stock Appreciation Rights

PEOPLE OFTEN CONFUSE PHANTOM STOCK with stock appreciation rights (SARs), with good reason—they are very similar.

For both types of arrangements, you are not receiving any equity in the company. Some companies, for example, do not want to dilute existing shareholders. This is especially the case with family-held businesses, which want to maintain control.

However, these companies realize that they need to motivate employees. With phantom stock and SARs, employees can benefit from the appreciation of a company's stock value.

With SARs, you have a contractual right to the appreciation of the stock value. Suppose you work for XYZ, a family business. XYZ grants you an SAR at $5 per share for 10,000 shares, vesting in two years. When two years elapse, the stock price is $15, so you decide to exercise your SAR. But you do not need to pay the exercise amount. Rather, XYZ will pay you in cash the difference between the grant amount and the current stock price, which is $10 per share, or a total of $10,000. You will pay ordinary income taxes on this amount.

For a phantom stock plan you can apply the same example, except that you receive the equivalent of $5 of stock at the time of the grant. After two years, you receive the $10 in appreciation, as well as the $5 of initial stock value, for a total of $15,000. Again, you must pay ordinary tax rates on this amount.

Be careful, though. Your company may not have the funds to pay for the phantom stock or SARs, perhaps because of liquidity problems. In other words, these plans really could be "phantom"! Ask your company if it has set up a separate fund to finance the phantom stock plan.

An employer might use a tandem SAR to help employees with the financial burden of exercising their stock options. This is a combination of an SAR and employee stock options. Basically, the cash from the SAR can be used to pay for the exercise of your options. Here are the requirements for SARs issued in tandem with ISOs:

➤ The SAR can be exercised only when the fair market value of the stock exceeds the exercise price of the ISO.
➤ The SAR cannot expire later than an ISO.
➤ The SAR is transferable only when the ISO is transferable.
➤ The SAR is exercisable only when the ISO is exercisable.
➤ The gain from the SAR may not exceed the value of the ISO.

Example: A year ago, you received an incentive stock option to buy 10,000 shares of your company for $10 each. You also received an SAR for 10,000 shares at $10 each. Both vest in one year and expire in ten years.

A year has elapsed, and the current stock price of XYZ is now $25. You exercise 2,000 shares of your SAR and receive $30,000 (2,000 times $15 per share). After this transaction, you now have 8,000 tandem SAR/ISOs.

Or you can use the SAR to exercise your ISO. Suppose you exercise 2,000 SARs and receive $30,000. You use the cash to exercise 3,000 shares of your ISO (3,000 times $10). You now have 5,000 left of your tandem SAR/ISOs (10,000 shares minus 2,000 SARs exercised and 3,000 ISOs exercised).

Let's say XYZ Corp. grants you nonquals for 1,000 shares with a $5 exercise price. You also get an SAR for 1,000 shares at $5. After one year, the 1,000 shares vest, and the stock price of XYZ is $10.

You exercise the nonquals and recognize a gain of $5,000 (1,000 times $5 per share), which is taxed at ordinary income tax rates. You also exercise your SAR and receive $5,000, which is also subject to ordinary income tax rates. Suppose that your federal income tax rate is 40 percent. You will owe $2,000 in tax for the nonquals and the SAR. But since you received cash from the SAR, you can use the after-tax amount, which is $3,000, to pay your tax liability on your nonquals. Thus, you need not sell your nonqual shares to pay for your tax liability.

Stock Grants versus Restricted Stock Grants

A COMPANY MAY GRANT YOU STOCK that vests immediately. This is reported as income for the year you get the grant, whether you sell the stock or not. For instance, your company grants you 1,000 shares of stock with a fair market value of $10 each. You will show gross income of $10,000 on your tax return. If you are considered an employee of XYZ, then your company will be required to withhold taxes from the $10,000. This amount can be taken out of your wages, or you can make the payment from your own cash holdings. The tax payment is a credit; it does not reduce the cost basis of the stock you own. Rather, the amount of income you recognized from the grant is the basis of your stock (that is, $10,000).

If you are not an employee, you are probably subject to self-employment taxes. This may require you to make estimated tax payments to avoid a penalty.

However, such stock grants are rare. A more common approach is restricted stock grants. That is, you will receive stock in the company if you meet certain restrictions, the most common of which is a vesting schedule. If you receive 10,000 shares of restricted stock with a two-year vesting schedule, then at the end of two years, provided you are still employed there, you have full title to 10,000 shares. At that time you will be taxed on the stock at your ordinary income tax rate.

Let's look at a real-life example. Merck, the pharmaceutical company, has a restricted stock plan. Each grant has a fixed term. If an employee leaves before it expires, then all restricted stock must be returned to Merck (although the company may make an exception and allow the employee to retain part of it).

On the certificate of the restricted shares is a legend that indicates the term of the restriction. The employee may not sell or dispose of the shares until the term expires. At that time, the legend is removed from the certificates. As a final note, Merck's plan states that no more than 6 million shares can be issued.

As a more specific example, Merck hired Raymond Gilmartin as CEO in June 1994, for a base salary of $1 million per year. When he left his former employer, Becton Dickinson, he forfeited a substantial amount of stock options. To compensate for this, Merck granted him 50,000 shares of restricted stock.

The restriction was in effect until June 1999. At that time, the stock had a value of $3.4 million. Gilmartin sold 18,225 shares in order to pay ordinary income taxes when the restricted shares vested.

Warrants

A WARRANT IS VERY SIMILAR TO a stock option. Like a stock option, a warrant gives the holder the right to buy stock in a company for a period of time. But there are differences. Warrants are usually given to major investors in a company. If, for example, you decide to invest $500,000 in a company, you may also get 100,000 warrants to buy stock in the company for $1 per share.

These warrants are called "equity sweeteners" and are used to persuade individuals or companies to invest in a company. For example, in June 2000, eToys raised $100 million from private investors, who received preferred stock with a 7 percent dividend. There were also warrants to buy 5 million shares of eToys common stock at $7.17 a share during the following three years.

In most cases, vesting does not apply to warrants. They can be exercised at any time. Also, warrants are not subject to a specific plan, such as a companywide stock option plan. Rather, they are negotiated on a case-by-case basis.

Warrants are taxed differently from stock options, because they are not used to compensate for services rendered to a company. Therefore, they are not taxed when exercised. Instead, you pay capital gains taxes when you sell the exercised stock.

Key Issues to Consider

➤ Your employer may offer you different ways to buy stock in your company, such as through a 401(k) or ESOP. But be careful; you do not want to have too much of your wealth tied up in your company's stock.

➤ You may be able to borrow from your 401(k) plan to pay for an exercise of a stock option. This may seem attractive, but there are pitfalls. For example, if you leave your job, you will probably have to pay off the whole loan immediately. If you don't, you will be subject to taxes on the withdrawal, as well as a 10 percent penalty.

➤ Some companies do not want to give out equity, so they will create incentive plans that act similarly to stock options. An example is a phantom stock plan. In this case, a company pays you cash based on the performance of the stock price. However, in some cases, a company may not have enough cash to pay its employees as promised.

➤ Exercising nonquals increases your ordinary income. This can be beneficial to your 401(k), because you might be able to contribute a higher amount. The contribution limit on a 401(k) is the lesser of $10,500 or 15 percent of your W-2 income.

➤ If your company grants you restricted stock, you could be subject to substantial taxes—whether you sell the stock or not.

Chapter Ten

Getting Your Share

THE TIGHT LABOR MARKET has made it easier for employees to get favorable pay packages. But this does not mean an employer will hand you a compensation package, complete with stock options, on a silver platter. You will need to engage in savvy negotiation.

The first step is to make sure your résumé and cover letters are top-notch and very professional. Also, make sure your cover letters are tailored to each prospective employer, demonstrating how your skills relate to the specific needs of the firm to which you are applying for employment. The more reasons you give the firm for hiring you, the more interest they will show in attracting you with stock options.

And never take the first offer. Wait at least a few days before deciding to work for a company. Companies usually have a great deal of latitude in granting stock options. If the employer offers 20,000 shares, you probably can negotiate for at least 50 percent more.

Number of Shares

YOU ARE A SOUGHT-AFTER Linux programmer in Silicon Valley. Every week you get at least ten job offers, but you finally narrow your choices down to two companies that you would like to work for: ABC and XYZ. Both are offering the same salary, but the options packages are very different. ABC is offering you stock options on 50,000 shares, while XYZ is offering you 100,000. Both have exercise prices of $1 per share.

The XYZ deal sounds tempting, right? Most people would choose this one, but they're forgetting an important element: how many shares does XYZ have outstanding? If ABC had 1 million shares outstanding, you would own 5 percent of the company. On the other hand, if XYZ had 10 million shares outstanding, your ownership of the company would be only 1 percent.

So before accepting the option offer, ask your company how many shares are outstanding and how many it is authorized to issue. Sometimes companies can issue 1 billion or more shares, raising the possibility that your shares could be diluted.

If your company is public, then the authorized and outstanding amounts will be disclosed in its proxy statements. If the company is private, this information can be difficult to get, although you can ask the company for a copy of its articles of incorporation. This will indicate how many shares the company is authorized to issue.

WestWard Pay Strategies, a compensation consulting firm, has a general formula for calculating dilution of a private company. The firm estimates that the average high-tech company will seek financing about every six months, and the dilution will be about 30 percent. Suppose you have 200,000 shares of XYZ, which is 2 percent of the company (the company has 10 million shares outstanding). It has another round of financing and issues 3 million new shares. Your ownership percentage would now be 1.5 percent.

Pay Ranges

THE INTERNET IS MAKING it easier to find information on standard pay scales. This can be a good starting point for negotiating your pay package. Also, you can find executive compensation in a company's filings with the Securities and Exchange Commission (assuming the company is public). Of course, you can uncover many other resources on the Web. Here are the top ones:

➤ **Exec-U-Net** (www.execunet.com). The site has information on salaries, options, and bonuses for about 650 management positions. The fee is $100.

➢ **FutureStep** (www.futurestep.com). This is sponsored by the executive recruiting firm Korn/Ferry. There is no fee.

➢ **JobSmart** (www.jobsmart.com). This aggregates 150 salary surveys that are posted on the Web. There is no fee.

Another strategy is to consult your advisers about the pluses and minuses in your pay package; these professionals can be great resources for determining appropriate option packages, and they can offer the tax, legal, and financial perspective you need.

Finally, you might want to visit some Web chat sites and ask other professionals for some benchmarks, guidelines, and overall anecdotal experience with stock option packages. For example, www.mystock-options.com has a discussion board on stock options.

Relocation

SUPPOSE YOU ARE OFFERED A tremendous compensation package, with plenty of stock options. Unfortunately, you live in New York, and the new job is in Los Angeles. Plus, you have three kids in grade school and a home with a big mortgage.

In these situations, you should negotiate to have the employer pay for your relocation expenses, including moving expenses and the closing costs of your new mortgage. Most important, stress to the company that you are making a big change and negotiate for extra consideration, such as additional stock options.

High-Risk Jobs

FOR THE PAST FIVE YEARS, you have worked for a publicly traded company. Every year, the stock price has increased about 30 percent. If you stay another year, you will have about $200,000 in options.

Now a private company wants to hire you. The company has a great deal of potential but many risks. In fact, the company is losing $1 million per month. If the product fails, the company will go bust. What's more, if you leave your current employer, you will forgo the potential $200,000.

In this type of situation, you should make clear to the employer what your concerns are. Underscore that the company's situation is iffy, that you would be giving up a great deal of value from your current employer, and that you should be compensated accordingly.

If the employer seems amenable, you can ask for a substantial options package as well as favorable vesting (for example, the options might vest over two years instead of four). Also, you could ask for a signing bonus, perhaps in the range of $50,000.

Creative Negotiation

YOU HAVE JUST GRADUATED from Stanford with a Ph.D. in computer science. Many fast-growing tech companies want to hire you, but you've set your sights on one company in particular, which is offering 100,000 shares as part of your compensation. You think a more reasonable amount would be 150,000. But the employer says, "You are definitely smart, but you haven't been proven. This is a good amount to start."

In such cases, you might want to propose a compromise—a package based on achieving certain goals. For example, if you develop a product ahead of schedule, you would receive an additional 50,000 shares. Also, ask if the company can make the vesting schedule more favorable—for instance, if the company initially offers you options that vest equally over a five-year period, you could ask them to shorten the vesting period to two years and then vest an equal amount every month thereafter. In other words, you get your shares earlier. This can be critical in the New Age economy, in which people move more quickly from one job to another.

Pay Cuts

THE TIGHT LABOR MARKET has made it possible for some people to wangle large option grants and large salaries at the same time. However, many companies are still resistant to this, especially young companies that need to conserve their cash.

Suppose you want to work for such a company, and your goal is to receive options for 100,000 shares. Unfortunately, the company offers you only 80,000 shares. But it can offer more options if you are willing to take a cut in salary.

You need to weigh the overall job opportunity against your

career goals, but if you do agree to make a cut, make sure the percentage increase in the options exceeds the salary-cut percentage, because options are risky, while cash is not. Thus, you might agree to take a 10 percent cut in salary, but only if you receive a 25 percent increase in options.

Reviews

ONCE YOU GET THE JOB, the negotiation does not stop. You want to make sure that your compensation reflects the work you do. When negotiating your employment, request more frequent review periods, such as every six months instead of every year. If you show exceptional achievements and productivity, you might be able to ask for additional stock options.

To maximize the potential raise or promotion, make sure you keep track of all of your accomplishments. Did you get a big client? Did you finish your project ahead of schedule? Did you develop a new idea? Did you save the company money?

In other words, base the increase on objective factors. One mistake is to compare your compensation to that of others in your workplace. Employers do not like employees to discuss their salaries with each other.

Now, let's say another company makes a very attractive offer. You should immediately talk to your employer. Point out your accomplishments and ask if something can be worked out, such as a renegotiation of your compensation. But never issue an ultimatum. This can cause a great deal of ill will if you do continue at your current job.

Of course, there are times you shouldn't bring up raises:

➤ If the company has new management, it will be difficult to prove your worth immediately.

➤ If the company is in trouble, it may well be inclined to actually terminate your employment rather than increase your compensation.

➤ And if you really haven't performed well, then no, it's not a good idea to ask for more compensation.

Personal Web Page

WEB PAGES AREN'T JUST FOR programmers and other technical people. More and more traditional employees have them, too. In fact, a personal Web page can be a great tool to set yourself apart, allowing you to elevate your profile in the marketplace and eventually put yourself in a position to negotiate more stock options. In fact, you do not even have to pay to get your own page. Here are two services that you can take advantage of:

1 **GeoCities** (www.geocities.com)
2 **Tripod** (www.tripod.com)

Your Internet service provider probably also offers free Web page services. These services are easy to use, giving you access to a myriad of tutorial information, as well as Web page creation tools. In less than an hour, you can be an official netizen.

If you do not want to create your own page, there are plenty of Web designers who will do it for you. Expect to pay anywhere from $200 to $5,000. While Web designers abound, finding a good one is not easy, so ask for references.

Put as many samples of your work on your Web page as you can. If you are a writer, include an article, report, or marketing piece. If you are an architect, show a building you designed. Just remember that an effective Web page is a simple one. You want a prospective employer to quickly understand your strengths.

Here are some other useful rules:

➤ Keep an up-to-date résumé on the site. Make sure companies can easily download and print it. And place the domain name of your personal Web page on every hard copy of your résumé.

➤ Have a hobbies section. This gives employers a little insight into you as a person. But try to correlate your hobbies with your professional skills. For example, if you coach your daughter's basketball team, highlight the leadership and communication skills that coaching embodies.

➤ Make sure your Web site loads quickly. Do not use too many graphics, because they can slow down your Web page and irritate prospective employers.

➤ Finally, remember to periodically update the site to keep it fresh.

Recruiters

IN MOST PROFESSIONS, recruiters are becoming key to career growth. Recruiting is a huge business that is growing very quickly as companies compete for top talent in a tight labor market. So when you get a call from a recruiter, take it seriously, and respond as soon as you can. A recruiter can be a valuable ally.

By definition, a recruiter is someone who seeks out qualified talent for companies. Recruiters are compensated in one of two ways:

Contingency. Here, a company pays the recruiter a commission if it hires one of the recruiter's candidates. If this type of recruiter calls you, you are probably one of many on a list of potential employees. Companies typically use contingency recruiters for positions paying less than $100,000 a year and for positions with many qualified candidates.

Retainer. Under this arrangement, a company pays a nonrefundable amount to have a recruiter find talent. If such a recruiter calls you, then you probably are a strong candidate. Retained recruiters usually are trying to fill positions that pay more than $100,000, and they are looking for individuals with very unique skill sets. These jobs often include stock option packages.

How can you tell which type of recruiter is calling you? The best approach is to ask. Ethically, a recruiter must disclose how he or she is being compensated. Also, ask the recruiter to send a brochure to you, and take a look at the firm's Web site.

If a recruiter requests payment from you, run the other way. The company pays for recruiting services, not the employee. Basically, a company is paying the recruiter to narrow the list of prospective candidates, which is a valuable service.

You should always be honest with a recruiter. Give accurate information about your prior job history and career goals. You don't want to waste a recruiter's time—or your own. Recruiters will usually check references and do background checks on candidates anyway.

Building strong relationships with recruiters can be very beneficial for your career, so make an effort to stay in touch with a few before you actually need them. You might want to send Christmas cards, help them with possible leads, take them to lunch, and so on.

To find good recruiters, you should do the following:

➤ Get referrals from others in your industry.

➤ Attend association meetings and conferences. Recruiters use these events to network.

➤ Review career sites (listed in Appendix A, Web Site Resources). You will quickly find out which ones are best for you.

➤ Seek out recruiters that have contacted you in the past.

Try to arrange meetings with firms that fit your criteria. In many cases you will not only submit your résumé, but also give an interview. If the recruiter does not call you back, do not take it personally. In most cases, the recruiter simply does not have a job that fits. But the recruiter will probably put your résumé in the database, so you might have another opportunity in the future when a more suitable job comes up.

Inquire about the policies of the recruiting firm. How do they handle confidentiality? Do they merely mass-mail your résumé? Do they prefer to be contacted via e-mail, phone, or fax? Try to get a feel for how the firm does business.

The following are top recruiting firms:

➤ Korn/Ferry

➤ Heidrick & Struggles

➤ Spencer Stuart

➤ Russell Reynolds

➤ LAI Worldwide

➤ TASA Worldwide

➤ A. T. Kearney

➤ Egon & Berndtson

➤ DHR International

Most firms specialize in one or two industries, so if the firm says that it is general-purpose, it's a danger sign that it is probably not effective. But do not focus solely on the top firms. Many small firms provide excellent service and can even offer certain advantages over large firms, such as more personal attention.

There are also purely Internet-based recruiting companies. As a prospective employee, you can submit your résumé free of charge for inclusion in their databases. Examples include the following:

➤ CareerCentral.com

➤ MBAFreeAgents.com

➤ CareerBuilder.com

Money Is Not Everything

SOMETIMES EMPLOYEES ALLOW OPTIONS to cloud their judgment because they regard them as a guaranteed path to riches. But if you watched Internet stocks plunge in 2000, you know that options can easily become worthless. Therefore, you should not sacrifice all of your other monetary considerations in order to maximize the number of options you receive. Rather, try to strike a balance with your overall compensation.

Moreover, getting the highest-paid job does not necessarily make sense for your career. For example, let's say you have two job offers. One has more stock options and a higher salary than the other. No-brainer, right? Well, the lower-paying job may provide more responsibility and greater experiences, which can lead to more rewarding job opportunities. Or the lower-paying job may be in an industry with faster growth prospects. Finally, don't forget about the "soft" benefits, such as vacation time, work-at-home programs, flextime, and an appealing company culture.

Along these lines, it is critical to determine what your priorities are. They may not be related to stock options or salary. Therefore, when you begin negotiating, deal with your main priorities first so that you don't waste your time in an overly long negotiating process.

You need to do lots of soul-searching and evaluate your ultimate goals. For instance, you may realize that you are in the wrong profession. Perhaps you really want to go to law school and become a lawyer. Be very candid with and about yourself. If you are not, your career prospects will be very limited.

Key Issues to Consider

➤ Never take the first offer. And wait at least a few days before deciding to work for a company.
➤ Many people look only at the number of shares of the option offer. However, what percentage does this represent of the company's outstanding stock?
➤ If your great job offer is in another state, make sure you get compensated for the relocation, and ask for more stock options.

➤ Leaving your current job may mean forgoing unvested options that have lots of potential value. In negotiating with a new employer, see if you can get extra options or a signing bonus to compensate for this.

➤ To get a good option package, you need to set yourself apart. Show your company how valuable you are. And be creative. One good idea is to create a personal Web site that highlights your professional accomplishments and skills.

➤ An employer may offer you more options in exchange for a pay cut. However, the labor market for skilled employees is tight. In many cases, you do not need to take a pay cut.

➤ Remember that money and stock options are not the most important things. After all, it is critical that you enjoy your work and that it advances your long-term career goals.

Section Three

Living with Stock Options

Chapter Eleven

Finding the Right
Advisers

W HEN IT COMES TO FINANCIAL PLANNING for your stock options, you should seek professional advice. If you make a mistake, say on your taxes, you could lose lots of money in stock options—perhaps millions of dollars. This is particularly true because the rules are constantly changing and complex. But if you can find a good adviser who specializes in the options field, you can maximize the value of your stock options.

To take an example, Jane has worked for a company for one year and has 10,000 shares that are vested in ABC Co. stock. She has met the requirements for an exercise of those shares to be treated as an incentive stock option (ISO), and thus she can be taxed at capital gains rates. She is in the top tax bracket (39.5 percent). The exercise price is $10, and the current market price is $20, which amounts to a $100,000 gain.

She decides to retire from the company and exercise all of her shares. According to the IRS, the maximum time in which she may exercise the shares and still have them considered incentive stock options is ninety days. However, some companies have a shorter time period, which is stated in the contract. Suppose ABC has a thirty-day time limit. If she exercises the options one day late, the $100,000 gain is treated as ordinary income, with a tax of $39,500 (39.5 percent times $100,000). If she exercises her options on schedule, the taxes are $28,000 (28 percent times $100,000). A good adviser can alert you to such potential problems. Even if you'd paid $5,000 for the advice, you still would have benefited.

Your Advisory Team

TO MAXIMIZE THE VALUE of your stock options, you need three basic types of services:

1 **Investment.** You need to create a financial plan that encompasses all of your assets, liabilities, and goals. The objective of the plan is to best allocate your assets by balancing risk and return. One of the biggest challenges is diversifying your stock options, because it is so common for the stock to represent a substantial percentage of your wealth. Clearly, if the value plummets, you can suffer some adverse financial consequences. A good financial plan takes this possibility into account and can incorporate several strategies for effectively diversifying your portfolio.

2 **Legal.** There are many legal aspects to options. These include termination, buyouts, acceleration of vesting, and noncompetition clauses.

3 **Taxes.** Tax rules for stock options are extremely complex. As shown above, by missing a deadline or by not complying with tax regulations, you can lose a substantial amount of money.

Because stock options are so complex and the regulations and laws governing them are still evolving, it is rare to find an adviser who can provide all of the necessary services. In fact, it is important to find specialists who will constantly keep up with the latest changes in their fields. The best strategy is to have three advisers: a financial adviser (also known as a planner or wealth manager), a CPA (certified public accountant), and a lawyer.

Get these advisers lined up as soon as possible. They will help build a foundation that maximizes the value of your options. And remember that it is critical to keep your advisers informed of any major life changes: divorce, new kids, a new job, or promotion.

Financial Advisers

IT IS PROBABLY NOT A GOOD IDEA to use a stockbroker as your stock option counselor. Stockbrokers are, for the most part, salespeople. They deal with forming portfolios, and in many cases, they do not have the necessary background to properly address the issues stock option plans create. It is better to have a financial planner. A good planner will take a holistic approach to your finances: tax planning, estate planning, insurance, retirement, investments, and employee benefits.

All good planners will first interview you extensively to identify and describe your goals and tolerance for risk. The planner will also gather your financial information, including wills, tax returns, mortgage, and partnership agreements. This can take weeks, and the initial expenses can be high ($5,000 to $10,000, or more). But it will be well worth the effort and expense.

The biggest mistake is opening the telephone book and selecting the first financial adviser you find. On the contrary, you should put a great deal of thought and effort into the process. Start by asking friends for referrals. Ask them some revealing questions, such as the following:

➤ What did you like about the adviser?

➤ Did your adviser help you with stock options?

➤ Was the adviser prompt in returning your phone calls and processing your transactions?

➤ Are you still using the adviser's services?

➤ What did you *not* like about the adviser?

➤ Did you trust the adviser? Do you feel he or she invested your money wisely?

➤ Do you feel you received good returns on your investments?

➤ Did the adviser pay attention to your level of risk tolerance?

Here are some other sources that can help you find a good financial adviser:

➤ **National Association of Personal Financial Planners.** This is an organization of experienced financial planners. Call the association at 800-366-2732.

➤ **Schwab AdvisorSource.** A specialist with Schwab will first determine your financial planning needs and then refer you to a local participating financial planner (who is not a Schwab employee). Schwab has stringent requirements: the planner must charge on a fee-only basis, have at least five years' experience, and manage at least $25 million in assets. For more information, call 888-774-3756. To qualify for the program, you must have a portfolio of at least $100,000.

➤ **Financial Planning Association.** This organization, formed January 1, 2000, is the result of a merger between the Institute of Certified Financial Planners and the International Association for Financial Planning. The FPA administers the certified financial planner designation, and its membership includes certified financial planners and others involved in the financial planning process, such as accountants, attorneys, money managers, and so on. For more information, call 800-322-4237 or visit the FPA's Web site at www.fpanet.org.

➤ **National Association of Personal Financial Advisors.** NAPFA is a professional association of 690 fee-only planners across the United States. (Fee-only planners do not accept commissions on the financial products they recommend to you.) For more information, call 888-FEE-ONLY (888-333-6659) or visit the association's Web site at www.napfa.org.

Some companies provide referrals to financial advisers, but be wary of this service. In many cases, the adviser's firm has a conflict of interest. For example, suppose that you have worked for XYZ for two years and it went public this year. XYZ used the brokerage firm J&J Advisers to handle the IPO. What's more, J&J also provides financial planning services. It would not be surprising if XYZ referred you to J&J. But since J&J handled the IPO, the firm would be motivated to persuade you not to exercise your options and sell your stock. Why? This may put pressure on the stock and reduce its value, which would lower the overall performance of the IPO and thus the firm's returns.

It is also common for the Wall Street firm to handle the cashless exercise of your options. Again, the broker handling the account may try to steer you away from exercising your options. Do not let this get in the way. Get outside, independent advice and avoid this sort of bias.

Once you pull together a list of good candidates for investment advisers, interview each of them. You can conduct the first interview by phone, which can be an efficient way to screen potential advisers. When you get several finalists, set up face-to-face interviews at each planner's office. By the way, you can use the same process when selecting a lawyer and CPA.

Key Questions to Ask Your Planner

How are you compensated? Financial planners use different types of compensation structures, including the following:

➤ **Commission.** This type of adviser receives sales commissions, fees, or "loads" on the products sold to you (usually a percentage of the amount you invest). There is a big conflict: The planner has the temptation to sell you the products that generate the highest commissions, not necessarily those with the best returns and risk profiles for your portfolio.

➤ **Fee-only.** Fee-only advisers may charge an hourly or a flat fee. Unlike the commission planner, a fee-only planner does not face conflicts about sales commissions.

➤ **Fee-based.** With this arrangement, a planner charges a flat fee but also receives commission compensation for some investment products you buy through him or her.

What are your credentials? At a minimum, make sure the financial planner is a certified financial planner (CFP), a designation administered by the Financial Planning Association. The requirements for the designation include at least three years' experience in financial planning, a college degree, and a passing grade on an intensive exam that lasts two days. CFPs must fulfill a thirty-hour continuing education requirement every two years. Currently, there are about 35,000 CFPs in the United States. To verify that a planner is a CFP and to check for possible disciplinary actions, you can call 888-CFP-MARK (888-237-6275).

Here are some other designations for financial planners:

➤ **Chartered financial consultant (ChFC).** This designation also covers many financial planning subjects, but from the perspective of a specialist in the insurance industry. A candidate must take eight comprehensive courses in financial planning and have three years of experience in the financial services industry. More than 32,000 people now have the designation, which was introduced in 1982.

➤ **Personal financial specialist (PFS).** A CPA typically is not trained to handle broad financial planning matters, but the PFS designation provides a strong background in dealing with the needs of people's personal finances. The designation is only for CPAs in good standing, with valid, unrevoked CPA certificates. The CPA needs a minimum of 250 hours of personal financial planning experience for three years. The candidate must then pass the PFS exam.

➤ **Chartered financial analyst (CFA).** This is for people who engage in sophisticated portfolio management. Getting the CFA designation is a long-term commitment. First, you need a minimum of three years' work experience. Then, over a three-year period, you must take three exams, which have a very high degree of difficulty.

➤ **Registered investment adviser (RIA).** While this sounds impressive, it really is not a strong indicator of investment advisory prowess. This is not a credential; rather, it is a designation that a person receives when he or she files certain forms with the Securities and Exchange Commission. It is required if the person wishes to charge for financial advice.

➤ **Certified equity professional (CEP).** This is a certification administered by the University of Santa Clara since 1989. It covers all aspects of employee options: securities laws, accounting, taxation, and plan administration. To get the accreditation, candidates must pass three exams. There are no education or work requirements.

How long have you been in the business? If the individual has been practicing for less than five years, be wary.

What is your area of expertise? Although good planners can provide comprehensive financial services, they typically have a specialty. More and more of them specialize in employee stock options.

What types of investments do you deal with? Are they conservative? Higher risk? What is your investment philosophy? How many investments do you typically recommend for a client? What kind of securities do you invest in? Do you personally research your own investments?

How often will you contact me? Do you use e-mail? When do I get account updates? What do they show? May I see a sample?

Do you have a sample financial plan?

What is your typical client like? Young? Older? Wealthy? How many of your clients have stock options? Can I contact some of your clients for references?

When interviewing potential advisers, also pay attention to these intangible aspects:

➤ **Personality.** Your adviser is the expert, but you're the boss, because you are the one paying the fees. If your first impression is negative and you feel a lack of chemistry, go to another adviser.

➤ **High pressure.** Avoid advisers who try to push you into hiring them. At the first meeting, the adviser should not be trying to close the deal.

➤ **Listening ability.** Is the adviser listening to you and addressing your concerns? Or is the person dominating the conversation?

When you have selected an adviser, get a letter from him or her outlining the specific services that will be provided. Also, put a time limit on these services, perhaps less than a month. Timing is crucial for stock options. If you ever have a dispute with the planner over unsatisfactory service, the letter can be powerful evidence in your favor.

Lawyers

LAWYERS CHARGE BY THE HOUR, and yes, it can get expensive. Rates range from $100 to $500 per hour (or more). Typically the best attorneys charge high rates, but they are more likely to provide better advice, and their expertise often enables them to spend less time on your situation than a rookie attorney would.

Referrals are usually a good source for locating a good lawyer. But you might also want to contact the local bar association and ask for attorneys who specialize in employee stock options. When interviewing a potential attorney, ask the following:

About how much will I pay for your services? Try to get a ballpark figure for generic legal services. If the attorney refuses to divulge that number, then go to another attorney.

What types of clients do you deal with? Are they mostly companies or individuals? This will help you determine whether the lawyer specializes in corporate or individual law.

Do you require a retainer? A retainer is an amount you pay to the attorney up front; this is a common arrangement. The attorney deducts his or her fees from the retainer as work is completed.

Will other individuals assist you in handling my legal affairs? Many attorneys have associates, who are typically young lawyers beginning their legal careers, or paralegals, who are usually quite knowledgeable about legal subjects but may not have a law degree. These individuals' rates are usually lower than the attorney's, but it's worthwhile to ask about their fees nevertheless.

When will you be done reviewing my documents? Finally, when you meet with your new lawyer about your stock options for the first time, make sure you bring the following: the employee handbook, all written correspondence with your prospective employer, contracts, and the option plan. Having complete information on hand helps the attorney give you the best advice possible.

CPAs

IN MANY WAYS, THE COMPLEXITIES of stock options revolve around tax issues, and the tax laws in this area are constantly evolving. If you had a gain from an incentive stock option, do you know on which line you should enter this information on your tax form? Even some CPAs do not.

To become a CPA, a person must have a four-year college education and pass an intensive exam. But not all CPAs are qualified to handle stock options. You need to find someone who has handled stock option situations before and knows the angles.

Some CPAs also become enrolled agents, a designation administered by the IRS. Note that a person need not be a CPA to become an enrolled agent. The requirements include passing a difficult two-day exam, plus seventy-two hours of continuing education credits every three years. Try to select a CPA professional who has this designation, because it is a specialty in taxation.

To locate CPAs in your area, you can contact the following organizations (ask which local members specialize in stock options).

➤ Licensed Independent Network of CPA Financial Planners (LINC, Inc.): 800-737-2727
➤ American Institute of Certified Public Accountants: 888-999-9256
➤ National Association of Enrolled Agents: 800-424-4339

When interviewing prospective CPAs, ask the following questions:

How many of your clients have stock options? What type of clients are they? Middle management? Programmers? Executives?

What are some examples of how you helped clients save money on taxes?

Do you focus only on stock options? If not, what proportion of your practice do stock options represent?

What types of journals do you subscribe to for understanding the latest developments in tax law for stock options? How much time do you spend reading them each week? Do you use online services? Do you attend conferences or take classes to keep up your stock option knowledge?

Examples of top employee stock option journals include *The Journal of Employee Ownership Law and Finance, The Corporate Counsel, American Compensation Association Journal, Benefits Quarterly, The Business Lawyer,* and *Compensation and Benefits Review.*

Do you use special software for stock option planning? This is essential. The tax calculations can be mind-boggling and require sophisticated financial modeling.

If I'm audited, will you represent me? If your CPA is an enrolled agent, he or she can represent your case before a tax court. An enrolled agent must either pass a two-day exam or work for the IRS for at least five years, regularly interpreting tax codes. It is the federal government that designates a person as an enrolled agent.

If I'm audited because of a mistake you made, will you pay for all of the costs? Do you have insurance to cover this?

Make sure you get these concerns addressed in writing. Ask the CPA for the certificate that indicates insurance coverage for errors and omissions.

Even if you've done your due diligence, you need to hold up your end of the bargain by keeping all of your records to get the most from your CPA. Make sure they are organized and easy for your accountant to handle. This will help to reduce your costs.

A quick note: Since you are seeking advice on compensation, the tax code allows you to deduct the fees you spend for advisory services. So make sure you keep the billing statements from your financial planner, lawyer, and CPA.

The Family Office

MOST WEALTHY PEOPLE HAVE their own full-time team of financial advisers. If you are worth several hundred million or more, it's to your advantage to do this, because even sophisticated investors need some guidance when dealing with this level of wealth. Unless you have a team of advisers, you are likely to be very confused about your financial situation. True, you may not be in this category right now. But then again, someday you might be.

This type of full-time advisory service is known as the "family office." For more information on creating a family office, contact the Family Office Exchange, an association of more than 900 family offices. The Web address is www.familyoffice.com.

Of course, our Internet-driven world now allows you to access the virtual family office. It is called, appropriately enough, myCFO.com. The company is the brainchild of Jim Clark, who has founded several highly successful companies—Healtheon, Netscape, and Silicon Graphics. As his wealth accumulated, he became dissatisfied with existing money managers. He wanted a better option, so he created myCFO.com.

With this service, each client gets a personal client-service representative, who is either a CPA or an attorney with more than a decade of experience. By logging on to myCFO.com, a client can get a comprehensive view of his or her portfolio.

The service handles all aspects of complex financial planning, such as tax structuring, estate planning, insurance, risk management, asset protection, bill paying, financial reporting, and charitable giving. It also offers integration of stock options.

Agents

HOLLYWOOD AND THE SPORTS INDUSTRY are not the only fields with high-powered agents. Now you can find top agents for high-tech executives and programmers. These agents will seek out the best job opportunities, and they will help craft the best compensation package, which can be crucial. How is an agent different from a recruiter? Well, a recruiter represents the company. An agent represents your interests solely.

Neal Lenarsky is one of the top agents. His firm, Strategic Transitions, is located in Woodland Hills, California. The Web address is www.sti-1.com. His firm specializes in positions in the entertainment, e-commerce, retail, and consumer goods industries.

In general, however, such agents are a new phenomenon, so it may not be easy to find one. They typically work by word-of-mouth. The best way to get an agent is to ask for referrals.

Conclusion

FINALLY, ALL OPTION PLANS HAVE an administrator, but all too often, few employees know about or tap this valuable resource. Ask your company who the plan administrator is so you can ask questions about the option plan. Most administrators keep up with the latest in the options field and are a good source of information. But be wary. An administrator should not be providing you with legal and financial planning advice.

Key Issues to Consider

➤ When managing your stock options, it is crucial to find a strong team of advisers: financial planner, lawyer, and CPA.
➤ It is critical to have advisers with a great deal of experience with stock options. Also, what types of clients do these advisers have? Are they programmers? Executives? It's ideal if your adviser has counseled people in your profession or industry before.
➤ While lawyers and CPAs must undergo years of education, there are few requirements for financial planners. However, there are a

variety of credentials—certified financial planner (CFP), char-
tered financial analyst (CFA), and chartered financial consultant
(ChFC)—that can set a financial planner apart from the rest of
the crowd. But be aware that some credentials, such as registered
investment adviser, have minimal requirements.
➤ Avoid advisers who are high-pressure.
➤ Get referrals. Also, ask your adviser if you can call existing clients.
This can be a good way to see how the adviser operates.

Chapter Twelve

Wealth Strategies

Y OU ARE A HOT-SHOT JAVA programmer for a Silicon Valley
start-up that went public last year. All told, your stock options
are worth $10 million and change. Even so, you still cannot
believe that you are a wealthy person. Up to now, you have always
lived modestly. You worked hard at school and then for your company. The payoff seems unbelievable, a dream come true.

When you achieve wealth, there are, of course, plenty of things to
worry about. Most important, you want to make sure you don't lose
your millions. This can happen in a variety of ways: lack of diversification; exposure to legal liability; and, yes, overspending.

In this chapter, we'll look at strategies for dealing with these
problems.

Asset Allocation

IT IS BECOMING MORE AND MORE COMMON for employees to have
large sums of wealth tied up in their stock options. In fact, options
and stock may become a person's biggest asset, and that presents a
problem: lack of diversification. Having most of your nest egg in a single company's stock leaves you with a high degree of portfolio risk. If
the employer's stock implodes, so does your wealth.

In other words, it is important to diversify away from large holdings of your company's stock. Bill Gates, who regularly sells shares of

Microsoft, is a prime example of this strategy in action.

With respect to your company, there are several types of stock market risks to be aware of:

Cyclical risk. Every industry goes into slumps. In fact, even a company that was doing relatively well compared to the rest of its industry will likely be depressed when the whole sector is not doing well. This is also known as industry risk.

Example: In 2000, the dot-com sector underwent a significant slump. Even top-tier companies like Yahoo! fell substantially in value. At the end of 1999, Yahoo!'s stock was at $216. By December 2000, the stock was at $28.

Company risk. This is the possibility that the company will not execute its business objectives and will fall behind. In some cases, a company could go bankrupt.

For instance, Value America was a hot Internet e-commerce company that had the backing of the founder of Federal Express, Frederick Smith, as well as a cofounder of Microsoft, Paul Allen. When the company did its IPO in April 1999, the stock price tripled, and many employees rejoiced in the surging value of their stock options.

But the company quickly ran out of money, and sales were below expectations. In August 2000, the company declared bankruptcy and closed its Web site. The shares are worthless.

Inflation risk. During the 1990s, inflation in the prices of goods and services was moderate. Yet over time, even moderate inflation can have a big impact on investments. If your company's stock price is increasing 10 percent per year and inflation is rising 5 percent per year, your real rate of return is 5 percent. Also, keep in mind that in times of high inflation, stocks in general perform poorly. The reason is that the government probably will increase interest rates to slow down the economy, and investors, anticipating that tighter money will constrain companies from expanding and growing their earnings, are less eager to own stocks.

Liquidity risk. This is the risk of encountering difficulties in selling your investment. It is a prevalent problem with stock in privately held companies, because there is no formal exchange on which to buy and sell the shares. What's more, even stocks that are publicly traded may present liquidity risk. Small companies in particular do not have much visibility and have low trading volumes. Penny stocks are notorious for carrying significant liquidity risk.

Market risk. There is an ever-present risk that the general stock market will fall in value and that good and bad stocks alike will go out with the tide. It has been more than fifteen years since the last prolonged plunge in the stock market. Still, the possibility that stocks could be depressed across the board just when investors need to cash them in is what motivates many investors to keep some of their holdings in bonds and money market funds instead.

Information risk. This is a common problem for owners of foreign stocks as well as New Economy stocks. Basically, information risk refers to the difficulty of getting solid information on these stocks. In the case of foreign stocks, the materials may be written in another language or published overseas. As for small stocks, there might be little or no coverage from stock analysts or financial journals. Companies involved in speculative or start-up enterprises, including biotech and new Internet businesses, can be difficult to analyze with conventional measures of earnings and cash flow.

Currency risk. This one applies solely to foreign stocks. Most countries have currencies that are traded on foreign exchange markets. The volatility can be high, in which case the rates of returns on investments can be affected greatly.

Example: Suppose you have options on 10,000 shares of XYZ, based in the United Kingdom, that are denominated in pounds. The exercise price is £10. After one year, all 10,000 shares vest, and you exercise the option. The fair market value of XYZ is £20. The current exchange rate is £1.5 for every $1. Translated into U.S. dollars, you have a gain of $66,666.66.

You wait six months, and the stock climbs to £25. However, the exchange rate is now £3 for every $1 (that is, the dollar has gained, as you can exchange $1 for more pounds). In this case, your XYZ stock is worth only $50,000.

Any one of these risks can have a substantial adverse impact on your stock options. If the company tanks, so will your stock options; if you work for a foreign company, you might be subject to currency risk; if you work for a private company, you have to contend with information risk or liquidity risk.

As an option holder, you need to find ways to minimize the risk to your stock holdings while maximizing your returns. For that, the first technique of choice is asset allocation. As the name implies, your asset allocation indicates what percentage of your wealth is in certain asset types. You might have 20 percent in real estate, 20 percent in stocks, 10 percent in bonds, and 50 percent in stock options.

In asset allocation theory, you reduce the overall volatility of your portfolio by changing the respective percentages of your assets. The idea is that if one asset decreases in value, another will be likely to rise or at least not drop as far or as fast. This helps to smooth out fluctuations in the value of your portfolio.

There are resources on the Web that can help you construct an asset allocation program. One of the best is from Fidelity, which manages the world's biggest mutual fund. The firm's online financial planner is at http://personal300.fidelity.com/planning/investment/. To construct your asset allocation profile, the computer program has a questionnaire, which covers investment time horizon, risk tolerance, and your personal financial situation.

According to the Fidelity methodology, the time horizon is the most critical factor, because the longer the time horizon, the more aggressive you can be with your asset mix. This means holding more options and stocks.

Asset Protection

IF YOU ARE READING THIS BOOK and have or hope to have a substantial amount of wealth, then you are going to be a potential target of lawsuits. This is known as the "deep pocket theory." That is, if something goes wrong—such as a car accident or an injury on your property—a person could stand to make a huge sum if he sues in court. Plaintiffs are more likely to sue because they have something to sue over: cash. The fact that you have money can also subject you to nuisance lawsuits.

Let's suppose you get sued and you lose, say, $5 million. You may be forced to sell your options and underlying stock to pay for the judgment, and you could face large tax penalties. The timing also may be bad if you have to sell the stock when the price is depressed. In light of the expenses of litigation, it often makes sense to settle—even if you know you are not at fault.

Lawsuits are only the most extreme threat to your hard-earned assets. When you become wealthy, you will eventually be barraged by aggressive stockbrokers and other financial advisers. Some of them will offer too-good-to-be-true techniques to shelter your income from lawsuits and creditors. These promoters will talk about the virtues of placing your money offshore, such as in the Cayman Islands. These are known as offshore trusts.

Let's take an example: You work in the United States and have vested options on 100,000 shares of XYZ stock. You exercise and then sell these shares, generating after-tax profits of $4 million. You then place this in an overseas trust. No sooner is the trust set up than you are involved in a car accident. After one year, there is a judgment against you for $3 million.

However, when the creditor tries to collect on the judgment, he discovers that most of your money is overseas. Not only that, but the country where your money is located has stringent rules about collecting judgments. For example, the country may have a one-year statute of limitations, which is common in overseas havens. In other words, a creditor has only one year after the event that precipitated the lawsuit (in this case, the car accident) in which to collect the judgment. Since U.S. court systems are fairly slow, a one-year statute is a major barrier to collecting U.S. judgments.

There are other barriers, too. The country may require a new trial, at which the creditor must appear in person. The creditor may also be required to prove his case "beyond a reasonable doubt." This is a much higher standard than "a preponderance of the evidence," which is the benchmark used in civil trials in the United States.

Sounds great? Well, offshore protection may not be a panacea. Here are some factors to consider before you ship all of your money to Bermuda:

➤ **Political instability.** The country where you keep your money may get a new government that disallows the laws on trusts and financial secrecy and hikes the tax rates as well.

➤ **Audits.** If you have an overseas trust, you must specify that fact on your U.S. tax return. But because of the substantial tax fraud potential that can surround overseas trusts, reporting one on your tax return is a red flag to the IRS.

➤ **Expenses.** Establishing an offshore trust can be expensive and complex. You need to create a corporation, which usually has setup and ongoing fees. There are also many administrative details, such as naming directors and having shareholder meetings.

➤ **Penalties.** If the overseas trust is not established properly and you take deductions that are disallowed by the IRS, you will have to pay back the taxes you owe plus interest and penalties.

This is not to imply that overseas trusts are all bad. Indeed, some can be very effective at protecting your assets. However, you will have to find and pay a qualified adviser who understands the many complexities and pitfalls of this tricky area. In general, a better strategy for protecting your assets is to get sufficient insurance.

Insurance

AS YOUR STOCK OPTIONS make you wealthier, you are likely to buy new assets, such as cars, homes, furnishings, electronics, and jewelry. If you want to make sure that your prized assets are protected from damage or lawsuits, you need to first make an inventory of your assets that records what each item is worth. Each time you acquire a new asset, add it to your inventory list. It is also a good idea to photograph or videotape the items.

Armed with your list, you can buy insurance to protect each of your main assets. For example, a home owner's policy will protect against personal liability (for example, your liability if someone gets hurt on your property), loss of the value of the real estate or personal property within the home, and loss of the use of your home.

If you have an expensive home (say, in excess of $500,000), consider buying "special-form" insurance. This provides for the broadest coverage, although it does not cover floods or earthquakes. If such events are a threat to your home, it makes sense to buy a separate policy to cover catastrophes.

If the personal property in your home is expensive, consider buying comprehensive personal property coverage. Suppose you bought a painting a few years ago for $5,000 that is now worth $100,000. If the painting is destroyed in a fire, a traditional policy probably will not cover it, or at least not its full value.

Finally, you may want to think about personal umbrella protection. This is insurance that goes beyond the limits of a home owners and auto policy to cover such events as a catastrophic accident involving your car, pool, boat, or vacation property.

True, this array of policies is a lot of insurance, and the premiums will seem high. Then again, it could cost more than you can afford to pay for lawsuits or a damaged house. You might be forced to exercise stock options that you would rather keep.

To balance the cost, you can increase the deductibles on your policies. A deductible is the amount you must pay before the insurance company will pay your claim. Higher deductibles tend to lower your premiums.

As a final note on the topic of insurance, do not neglect the important (although unpleasant) subject of disability. For people under fifty, it is far more common to be disabled than to die. Your employer may provide you with disability insurance, which typically covers 60 to 70 percent of your income. Or you can buy a private policy.

However, keep in mind that your policy probably will not cover your employee stock options, because disability insurance covers only earned income sources. Therefore, if you lost your job because of a disability, you would lose any unvested stock options.

It has been argued that the same logic that applies to insuring intangible assets could also apply to stock options, so it is possible that an insurer will develop a policy covering stock options someday. In the meantime, to cover yourself, you could try to negotiate a clause in your option agreement that part or all of your options would vest if you became disabled.

Hedging

SUPPOSE THAT TWO YEARS AGO you joined your company as the vice president of marketing. You received a substantial deck of options: 200,000 shares, with an exercise price of 10¢ per share. Several months ago, the company went public. The stock price is now $50 per share, and your options are worth about $10 million.

However, the stock does not see a large amount of daily trading volume. If you tried to sell 200,000 shares immediately, you would probably affect the stock price. Also, since you are a vice president of marketing, you will have to report all of your stock sales. If you decided to sell all of your shares, it would look as if you had lost your faith in the company, which might depress the stock price.

But you still fear that the stock may fall in value. Brokerage firms devised hedging strategies for this very purpose. They use derivative products—known by such exotic names as collars and swaps—to lock in your gains. The downside of using such strategies is that you usually will not be able to participate in any further stock gains. Let's look at the different strategies available to you.

Short Selling

SHORT SELLING ALLOWS YOU to make money when a stock falls in value. For instance, you think your company's stock price will plunge, so you sell short 1,000 shares. The current stock price is $20. In the transaction, you basically reverse the buy-and-sell process. That is, you first sell the 1,000 shares, generating proceeds of $20,000 (1,000 shares times $20 per share). The amount is then escrowed.

You wait a year, and the stock is now selling for $5 per share. You then buy the 1,000 shares for $5,000 and turn them in to close out the short sale. The difference is your profit: $15,000 ($20,000 minus $5,000).

However, suppose the stock went to $40. In that case, you would buy back the shares at $40,000 and then turn them in to close out the short sale. In that case, you would lose $20,000 ($40,000 minus $20,000).

In a way, the potential losses from a short sale are unlimited. After all, what if you had sold short Microsoft ten years ago?

You can use short selling as a hedging technique. For example, suppose you have 1,000 options in XYZ, with an exercise price of $10. You exercise the options for $10,000. Although you do not want to sell the stock, you fear that it could fall. You could sell the 1,000 shares short, essentially locking in a price of $10. Thus, if the shares increase in value, the short sale position will decline accordingly, and vice versa. This is called "shorting against the box."

But using a short-sale technique is not ideal, especially for ISOs. This is because the short sale will make the transaction a disqualifying disposition, assuming you do not meet the holding requirements. Also, a short sale will restart the holding period for capital gains treatment.

For example, you exercised 10,000 shares and held them for ten months, and then you shorted against the box on the shares. Three months later, you close out your position on the company by turning in your 10,000 shares to cancel the short sale. In this case, the transaction would be considered a short-term capital gain. To turn it into a long-term capital gain, you would have to hold the 10,000 shares for more than one year from the date of the short sale.

Finally, you need to be aware of something else: constructive sale. If you have a large gain locked up from a short sale, the IRS will make you recognize the gain by January 30 of the year following the short sale. To avoid this, you will need to close your short-sale position and hold your stock for at least sixty days.

Protective Put

SOME PUBLIC COMPANIES WILL ALLOW investment options to be bought and sold on a stock exchange (usually on the Chicago Board Options Exchange). There are two methods you can use:

1 **Call.** Allows you to buy 100 shares of a stock during a period of three months for a fixed price (known as the strike price). If the stock price of the call increases above the fixed price, the value of the call option will also increase.

2 **Put.** Allows you to sell 100 shares of a stock during a period of three months for a fixed price. If the stock price of the put option falls below the strike price, the value of the put option will also decrease. (The purchase price of a put or call is called the premium.)

Some option holders use a strategy known as the "protective put." As an example, let's say you have 1,000 shares of a stock currently trading at $60 per share. You do not want to sell the shares, but at the same time, you are concerned that the stock may fall. Therefore, you buy 10 puts (a total of 1,000 shares) for a premium of $5 per share of the contract. The transaction costs $5,000 (1,000 times $5). The strike price of each put is $58.

Basically, with this protective put, the value of your portfolio will not fall below $58 per share. If the stock price does fall below this amount, the value of your puts will increase by the same amount, and vice versa. On the other hand, if the stock soars, there is no limitation on the upside.

But remember that the protection is only for three months. Also, there could be adverse tax consequences; that is, the holding period of your shares may be restarted or, in the case of ISOs, you may trigger a disqualifying disposition. These scenarios are likely if the put is in-the-money. This means that the current stock price of the put is lower than the strike price.

Covered Call

IN A WAY, A COVERED CALL WRITING is a partial hedge for your stock holdings. Instead of buying a call, you sell it. Basically, in the deal, you are agreeing to sell your shares at the strike price, and for this, you receive a premium.

Example: You have an option for 10,000 shares of XYZ. You exercise the option. The current stock price is $40. You write an option for $45 per share, with a premium of $3. Therefore, you get $30,000 ($5 times 10,000 shares).

After three months, the call will expire. If the XYZ stock price is below $45, then the call will expire worthless. What's more, you have $3 of downside protection, since this was the premium you received from writing the call.

But if the stock does rise above $45, it will be exercised, and your 10,000 shares will be sold at $45 per share, for a total of $450,000. Including the premium of $30,000, you made $480,000.

The example above uses an out-of-the-money covered call. That is, the stock price is below the exercise price. You could also do an in-the-money covered call. These typically have higher premiums because there is intrinsic value to the option (intrinsic value is the difference between the exercise price and current stock price). But for an ISO, the in-the-money covered call may trigger a disqualifying disposition. Moreover, the capital gains holding period may be restarted.

Exchange Funds

EXCHANGE FUNDS ARE FOR THOSE who have substantial amounts of stock. So if you exercise your options and have at least $500,000 in stock, you should be eligible for an exchange fund.

If you transfer $500,000 of your exercised stock into an exchange fund, the transfer is considered tax-free and is put in a limited partnership. The limited partnership invests in a diversified portfolio of stocks and bonds (the fees are similar to those of a mutual fund). But you probably will be required to hold the money in the fund for at least two years.

Beware: There is speculation that Congress may crack down on exchange funds. If so, the tax consequences are unpredictable. After all, Congress has been known to undo tax breaks, especially during the 1980s, when it eliminated many tax shelters.

Collars

ONE OF THE MOST COMMON and useful hedging strategies for option holders is the costless collar. As the name implies, this strategy sets a range around the possible stock price movements. For example, let's say for XYZ stock, you place a collar between $60 and $90 per share. If the stock price goes above $90 per share, you are guaranteed this gain. If the stock falls below $60, you are guaranteed not to fall below $60.

Companies usually disapprove of such strategies because they want to keep you motivated with stock incentives. If the hedge is limiting the upside, the employee has less incentive to go all-out. And the well-hedged employee is not as concerned if the stock falls, either.

Margin

MARGIN IS THE USE OF STOCK as collateral to get a loan. Depending on your brokerage firm, you also might be able to use stock options as collateral.

Typically, a brokerage firm will loan up to 50 percent of your collateral. But the percentage depends on a variety of factors, such as the stability of the stock, the trading volume, and the stock price. For example, most firms will not margin a stock that is selling below $5 per share.

Now, a margin is not a hedge. But it can be used as a diversification tool. Let's say you exercise 100,000 options with an exercise price of $10. The current stock price is $100, so your stock is worth $9 million. You decide to take a margin loan of $1 million. With this, you make other investments, such as mutual funds.

This may sound very appealing, and it's a strategy that works well for many people. But bear in mind that using a margin loan to exercise employee stock options can be tricky—and risky. An article by John Barringer, "Stockbroker's Secrets: What I Only Tell My Best Clients About Option Exercise Strategies," that appeared recently on the Web site myStockOptions.com, illustrates the dangers. According to the article, in order to get a margin loan, the exercise price of the option must be at least 50 percent lower than the current market price of the underlying stock. If you have an option to exercise 1,000 shares of XYZ at $10, with a market price of $20, a broker will extend a margin loan for $10,000 to exercise the option.

But don't forget that you must pay monthly interest on the loan. If you cannot meet the payments, you must sell your shares to pay off the loan. What's more, if the stock falls below a certain point established by your broker, you will need to deposit more funds with the brokerage to cover your loan. This is called a margin call. If you do not deposit more money, your shares will be sold to pay off a portion or all of the loan.

On the bright side, the use of a margin does not trigger a taxable event, nor does it trigger a disqualifying disposition for ISOs. In fact, margin interest payments are tax deductible (that is, they are offset against any income from dividends or interest). Plus, a common tax strategy is to hold on to the exercised stock for at least one year to ensure that you are eligible for capital gains treatment. Of course, if the stock is not sold in the same year the option is exercised, you are subject to AMT.

Key Issues to Consider

➤ You may have a substantial amount of your wealth tied up in stock options. If the stock collapses, it could be disastrous. So remember to diversify your holdings into other assets.

➤ If you have a great deal of wealth from stock options, you may be a target for lawsuits. A great way to protect your wealth is making sure you have adequate insurance.

➤ There are many techniques to protect your stock options from plunging in value, such as hedging. Techniques include exchange funds, costless collars, protective puts, and covered-call writing.

➤ You may be able to borrow against your stock options through a margin loan from your brokerage firm. But beware: You must pay interest on the loan. And if the stock price plunges, you could potentially lose all of your gains because you are forced to sell stock to pay for your loan.

Chapter Thirteen

Serving as an Adviser or Consultant

F OR THE PAST TEN YEARS, you have worked on a variety of large-scale software projects for Oracle. It has been an exhilarating experience, and you have learned many lessons along the way. You meet a friend, Jack, who has decided to form his own high-tech company. He has raised $150,000 and is hiring a few programmers to begin work on the company's product. However, he needs advice on managing the project. Any missteps could be disastrous for the fledgling company. Jack asks you for advice and even suggests you serve on the advisory board.

With more and more small businesses springing up, chances are good that you will be offered advisory or consulting roles to some of them. You may well be flattered and intrigued, but before you agree to serve on a board or sign a contract to provide consulting services, you should take certain considerations into account.

Types of Boards

THERE ARE TWO TYPES OF BOARDS: the board of directors and the advisory board. While the advisory board is optional for a company, the board of directors is not. The board of directors provides broad decision-making for a company, such as declaring dividends, voting for a merger, or approving a stock option plan.

To facilitate decision-making, a board of directors is typically limited to anywhere from three to ten members. Advisory boards, on the other hand, may have a large number of people, sometimes more than twenty. The main reason is that the advisory board does not have any legal decision-making powers. Rather, as the name implies, the role is to provide advice to the company.

For example, Internet Capital Group (ICG), which invests in business-to-business companies, has an advisory board that consists of seventeen diverse members. They include Geoffrey Moore, the author of *Crossing the Chasm;* Sergio Zyman, former vice president and chief marketing officer of Coca-Cola; and John McKinley, the chief technology officer of Merrill Lynch. In contrast, the company's board of directors consists of seven members.

Option Compensation

INDUSTRY EXPERIENCE CAN BE a highly valuable asset, so do not give it away. You should get compensation. Until the 1990s, the compensation of boards of directors was mainly in the form of cash. A typical package would include a retainer, a fixed annual amount ranging from $5,000 to $100,000, whether the member attends the board meetings or not; meeting fees for attending meetings, ranging from $100 to $10,000 per meeting; insurance and pension benefits; and perks, such as discounts on company products.

These days compensation for directors on boards is increasingly based on stock options, mainly because shareholders want to tie the performance of board members to the value of the company. And advisory board positions are compensated almost solely through stock options.

For the most part, a company that is backed by a venture capitalist or publicly traded will likely have a standard compensation package for its board of directors and advisory board members. Thus, it can be difficult to negotiate terms. In fact, it is typically the case that people join boards for reasons other than money. After all, a board position is prestigious, as well as a great learning experience.

Sometimes board members do have the leverage to negotiate sizable compensation packages. Take Michael Jordan, the former all-star basketball player for the Chicago Bulls. He is a director of Oakley, a fashion eyeglasses company. Jordan has an agreement to receive an annual retainer of $500,000 and stock options to buy 217,392 shares at $11.50 each. But keep in mind that he is also obligated to endorse the company's products.

If you take on extra duties, you should ask for more stock options. Company boards usually have different committees that address broad corporate governance issues. Standard committees include compensation, which reviews executive salaries, incentive compensation, stock plans, benefits, and bonuses; budget, which reviews the company's finances, cash flow, financial projections, and so on; and audit, which reviews the professional services provided by the company's accountants.

If you are an officer of a company and a board member, it would be rare for you to get compensation for serving as a director (in this instance, you are called an inside director). Instead, your compensation will be based on the employee stock option plan. The options will likely be ISOs.

If you are a nonemployee director, then you will be granted nonqualified stock options. Many companies have a plan specifically for directors. Two examples are listed in the box on the following page.

Note: For public companies, director compensation must be disclosed to shareholders. The information is found in a company's proxy statements, which are known as section 14(a) filings. The company must disclose the terms of the plan as well as the compensation packages of all the directors. Looking at the 14(a) filings can be a great research tool.

If you are asked to be a board member or adviser of a pre-venture-capital private company, you have much negotiating leeway. A company at this stage usually does not have much savvy in drafting compensation arrangements. This is not to say that you should be opportunistic, because this will backfire. Your reputation for being a solid adviser is very important for your career growth.

How much do advisers and board members receive in the early stages of a company? According to Tim Bei, the director of business development at internet.com: "At the early stages, we generally see ranges between 0.05 percent and 0.08 percent on a fully diluted basis."

Of course, if you can bring a great deal of added value to a company, both you and the company will benefit. You should understand

Nonqualified Stock Options Plans for Nonemployee Directors

HERE ARE TWO EXAMPLES of nonqualified stock option plans for outside directors:

➤ **Red Hat.** This company is a leading provider for the Linux operating system. Once appointed to the board of Red Hat, directors receive options to buy 20,000 shares of common stock at the fair market value of the shares on the date of the grant. The options are nonqualified. The options vest 33.33 percent one year from the grant and 8.33 percent at the end of each three-month period thereafter. If reelected to the board, the director will get 10,000 more nonqualified options that vest on the same terms.

➤ **Maxygen.** This company is a leader in the emerging field of directed molecular evolution, a process in which genes are modified for commercial uses. In the directors' stock option plan, 300,000 shares were reserved, and each director gets a grant of 20,000 shares. At the first board meeting following each stockholders' meeting, there will be an additional grant of 5,000 shares. The company has the right to repurchase the shares—except for 25 percent of the shares one year after the date of grant and 25 percent of the shares at the end of each year thereafter.

the needs of a company in its early stages of development. Says Bei, "Top management at start-ups spend a large percentage of time looking for financing and view board advisers and directors as inroads to venture capitalists or angel investors. I would guess this is the single most important factor for choosing a board adviser."

The Duties

SERVING AS A BOARD MEMBER is no easy task. You need to maintain much knowledge about the company, and you might also need to travel if the company is in another state. Before joining a board, think about whether you have the necessary time and skills to contribute to the company.

In terms of liability, a member of the board of advisers has minimal liability. There is no fiduciary responsibility to the shareholders.

But a great deal of law does exist on the duties of a director. A director is a fiduciary; that is, he or she is responsible for the property of another. Therefore, a director has a duty of loyalty and a duty of care for the company. Breaching these duties can result in legal action.

This does not mean a director is not allowed to make mistakes. On the contrary, directors are encouraged to take risks. In fact, a legal doctrine called the "business judgment rule" provides much discretion for a company's board. In general, courts do not want to substitute their decisions for those of the directors. Therefore, as long as directors do their homework and attend their meetings, the business judgment rule applies, provided they exhibit reasonable judgment. This was not the case, however, with TransUnion Corp., whose board took only two hours to approve a big merger. The courts disallowed the business judgment rule.

Another problem area for directors is self-dealing, which calls the corporate opportunity doctrine into play. For example, if you have an opportunity to buy a software company and you are a director of a competing company, you must first present the offer to the board.

There are other types of conflicts you should be aware of. Suppose you are the banker to a company that has named you to the board. You may be tempted to relax your terms when extending a loan to the company. To deal with conflicts, it is a good idea to abstain from the vote and disclose your interests. Also, get legal counsel if you have any doubts about a situation presenting a conflict of interest.

Liability

THE JOB OF A DIRECTOR has become increasingly complex. A director will often deal with mergers and acquisitions, strategic ventures, and so on. If these deals blow up, lawsuits are likely to follow. Unfortunately, directors may be personally liable, and the suits can be for millions of dollars. In our litigious society, these suits have been increasing at an alarming rate. In fact, many people will not take board seats because of the legal environment.

There are many areas in which a board member can be liable:

➤ **Employees.** This is one of the most common areas of liability. Suits may involve such issues as termination, layoffs, racial discrimination, and sexual harassment.

➤ **Environmental.** Some industries, such as semiconductors, are prone to environmental liabilities. The judgments can be huge, and they can wipe out a company (the asbestos cases against the Johns Manville Corp. were a classic example).

➤ **Shareholders.** If the company's stock price falls greatly, then shareholders are likely to sue. Other areas of liability could be mergers and acquisitions and not disclosing material information.

➤ **Customers.** These suits usually entail contract disputes or trade practices.

Thus, many companies will take measures to protect directors, including the following:

➤ **Indemnification.** This means that in the event of a lawsuit, the company will pay for any damages.

➤ **Insurance.** Known as directors' and officers' (D&O) policies, this protection insures directors for a certain amount in the event of a lawsuit against the company.

In the bylaws of Looksmart, a compressive online directory that went public in 1999, directors and officers of the company are indemnified from liability to the "fullest extent permitted by law." Looksmart has also bought insurance to cover its directors; the policy covers such expenses as attorneys' fees, judgments, fines, and settlement amounts.

So before joining a board, make certain you find out the following information:

➤ **Type of policies.** Claims-made policies cover claims made while the policy is in effect. Liability-incurred policies cover claims incurred while the policy is in effect. In other words, claims can be filed while the policy is in effect, but they may also be filed later, as long as the event the policy is insuring against happened during the policy period. You have the most protection when the company provides both types of policies.

➤ **Amount.** How much will the policies cover? Remember, the judgments can be huge. Many policies cover more than $100 million, so keep that in mind as a benchmark.

➤ **Deductibles.** Policies usually require deductibles. Will you have to pay these in the event of a lawsuit, or will the company pay?

➤ **Employment practice liability.** Make sure the company has an insurance policy for this. An EPL policy covers sexual harassment and racial discrimination lawsuits, such as the landmark $100 million judgment against Texaco for race discrimination.

➤ **Cancellation.** Make certain the policy is noncancelable by the insurance company.

➤ **Reimbursement.** Some policies have a "reimbursement clause." This means that a director must pay the settlement or judgment from a suit, and then the insurer will reimburse the director for the expenses. But most directors do not have the available cash to make such payments. What's more, the reimbursement may occur more than six months after the director makes the payment. A better clause is "pay on behalf of," in which the employer pays the settlement on your behalf, thus avoiding the reimbursement issues.

Because of the liabilities involved, it's a good idea to have an attorney review any troublesome issues before you join a board. Also, you should check the status of the company's D&O insurance every year. Of course, D&O insurance does not cover everything. If the board has engaged in intentional actions that defrauded the company, then no D&O policy will cover the resulting lawsuits or damages. Examples include cooking the books, bribery, embezzlement, securities fraud, insider trading, price fixing, and so on.

High-Profile Board Members

HERE ARE SOME INTERESTING examples of well-known directors and a look at their compensation arrangements.

➤ **Jack Kemp**, a New York congressman for eighteen years, is on the board of Oracle, a leading software company. For his duties, Kemp is paid an annual retainer of $30,000, as well as $1,500 for each meeting and $2,000 for special meetings. He also received a grant of options to buy 75,000 shares.

➤ **Lester Thurow** is a director of E*TRADE, a leading online brokerage firm. He has been a professor of management and economics at the Massachusetts Institute of Technology and is also the author of several best-selling books on economics. He receives $5,000 per year and $800 for each meeting. He also got a grant of options to buy 80,000 shares.

Advisory Boards and Conflicts of Interest

LISA HAS RECENTLY STARTED a new company. She has raised $20 million and is building sophisticated equipment for fiber-optic networks. You work for a major telecom company that would be a potential customer for Lisa. She asks you to join the company's advisory board. In exchange, she offers 100,000 shares with an exercise price of 10¢.

You agree. Of course, you introduce Lisa to your employer, who subsequently agrees to buy $100 million in products over the next five years and also invest $40 million in the company.

Is this allowed? Surprisingly, this is a gray area. There is no case law on the matter. But if such an opportunity does arise, it is probably a good idea to seek counsel. Also, make sure you talk to your employer. Your company may have a policy against employees serving on the advisory boards of potential customers.

Hanging Out Your Consulting Shingle

ESPECIALLY FOR FAST-GROWING private companies, hiring consultants is becoming more and more common. These companies need expert advice, but a private company is usually short on cash. One way to reduce cash fees is to use stock options.

As a consultant, you are likely to advise several companies each year. Thus, you can—in a sense—build a diversified portfolio of equity positions in companies. If only a few do well, the rewards can be tremendous.

An example is Randy Komisar. His business card describes him as "Virtual CEO." He steps in as acting CEO for a start-up, organizing the company and launching the technology. He has done this with such companies as Magnifi, Digital IQ, Mondo Media, and WebTV. Then he steps aside as a permanent CEO comes on board. Of course, as part of his assignments, he takes substantial option positions in the start-ups.

Although all this sounds glamorous, you still need to be careful when you are considering taking options in start-ups. If you think the company has a questionable business model, then it is probably better to take cash. See Chapter 7 for factors to look for in identifying strong private companies.

Beware: Many private companies are led by overly optimistic CEOs. They will say things such as, "We'll do our IPO in six to twelve months." Unfortunately, this rarely happens. So when taking stock options, do not rely on them for immediate value. Make sure that you have the necessary savings to meet your living needs. You can't pay your bills with stock options!

Rock-Solid Contract

SUPPOSE YOU GET A NICE consulting agreement for XYZ Corp. It lasts for six months. You are to receive $30,000 in cash and 10,000 options to buy the stock at $1 per share after a one-year vesting period. But the company then reneges on the offer.

Depending on your contract, you might not have any recourse to the options. In fact, many consulting contracts contain a clause specifying that the options can be revoked for any reason.

One way to avoid this problem is to have a portion of your options vest every month. Another good strategy is to hire an attorney to help you determine whether you have a good case against the company. See Chapter 11 for more information on selecting a qualified attorney.

Examples of Consulting Arrangements

THE FOLLOWING ARE SOME EXAMPLES of consulting agreements involving stock options.

Xoom.com (XMCM). The company, a Web portal that was bought by NBC, went public at $14 per share in December 1998. Jeffrey Ballowe, who had been president of the Ziff-Davis Interactive Media and Development Group, hired on as a consultant to the company.

Ballowe had an ongoing consulting fee arrangement with Xoom.com for $10,000 per month, payable in stock options with a strike price of $4.50 per share. The options vested monthly over a two-year period. In the event of an IPO, all his shares would vest. Moreover, for any money he raised personally for Xoom.com, he received a 5 percent commission that was payable in stock options.

AboveNet (ABOV). Based in Silicon Valley, Stephen Belomy had become an expert in the real estate business. He landed AboveNet, an Internet service provider, as a client in 1996. For his services, he got an option for 104,166 shares with an exercise price of 12¢. He then decided to take a position as executive vice president of the company in 1997. The company went public in 1999 and then was sold to Metromedia Fiber Network for $1.2 billion.

Cobalt Networks. Gordon Campbell founded a firm, Techfarm, that provides advisory services for high-tech start-ups. He has held positions with Honeywell, Intersil, Intel, and Motorola, and his innovations include the first electronically erasable microcomputer and the first PC on a chip.

Campbell worked as a consultant for the successful start-up Viavision. The objectives of his contract with Viavision were clear:

(a) Assist Viavision in the development of a structure and strategy in order to obtain outside funding

(b) Assist Viavision in finalizing its business plan, including financial data and strategic issues related to the definition, development, marketing, and distribution of Viavision's products

(c) Assist in implementation of the strategic plan, including bringing the products to market and establishing strategic relationships

(d) Provide early-stage management, as needed, to round out Viavision's existing management expertise

(e) Make a representative of Techfarm available to serve on Viavision's board of directors

In the deal, Techfarm got $5,000 per month, although the payments were accrued until the company received financing.

When Techfarm arranged for the financing, 80 percent of the stock was slated for the founders and employees. The shares would be part of a stock option plan, with a vesting period of four years. Then Techfarm would get 20 percent of Viavision, also subject to a four-year vesting period. In the event of a change of control or IPO, all of the shares would be immediately vested.

Viavision changed its name to Cobalt Networks. The company did complete its IPO and was sold to Sun for $1.3 billion.

Global Crossing. Former President George Bush gives many speeches each year, typically charging $80,000 per appearance. But when he spoke to Global Crossing, which owns an undersea fiber-optic system, he took his fee in stock options. At one point, the options were worth more than $15 million.

Key Issues to Consider

➤ Joining the board of directors of a company or its advisory board is no easy task. You are likely to spend plenty of time with the company.

➤ As a member of the board of directors, you are subject to liability exposure (for example, if the stock price of the company collapses, you may be named in a lawsuit). It is important that the company has the necessary directors' and officers' (D&O) insurance policies to protect you.

➤ When negotiating a board seat or an advisory position, you have much more leeway when dealing with early-stage companies. By the time venture capitalists enter the deal, your option package probably will be standardized.

➤ Serving as a member of the advisory board or even the board of directors can present conflicts of interest. Before joining a board, talk to your current employer to make sure you have its approval and to keep everything aboveboard.

➤ If you are a consultant to a company, you might want to ask for stock options. However, keep in mind that you need a rock-solid contract. In many cases, a company has the ability to renege on your options. One idea is to request monthly vesting of your stock options.

C h a p t e r 14 *u r t e e n*

Divorce

S INCE 1960, WHEN 2 out of every 1,000 marriages ended in
divorce, the laws governing divorce and the division of property have changed dramatically. Today, with an estimated one-half
of all marriages ending in divorce, the legal system has in many
respects kept pace with division-of-property issues but also has
become increasingly complex.

Dividing books and furniture is easy. Dividing real estate is more
difficult, but deciding who is entitled to own which portion of the
stock options package is arguably the most challenging task. In addition to the difficulty of determining the value of the options, it is often
unclear who should realize the benefit of any appreciation in value.

To further complicate matters, the holder of the options often
must continue to work to obtain the benefit of the options. When the
options vest, the price of the stock could soar, plunge, or tread water.
This ambiguity has given rise to uncertainty, anxiety, and, in the worst
cases, litigation.

A high-profile divorce in 1997 highlights the complexities in this
area. Gary Wendt, former chief executive officer of General Electric
Capital, decided to end his marriage of more than thirty years. He
held many stock options in his company. His wife, Lorna, claimed a
$100 million ownership interest in the options. Mr. Wendt disagreed
but offered $11 million to settle the issue. A Connecticut Superior
Court awarded Mrs. Wendt a judgment for $20 million in an acrimo-

nious family law dispute that will likely reverberate for some time.

This chapter introduces the significant issues posed in a divorce when one or both of the parties hold stock options. Although summaries of the law and issues are presented here, this chapter is no substitute for qualified legal and accounting counsel, which is almost always necessary.

Who Owns What?

CRITICAL TO ANY DIVORCE is determining who owns what. Of course, this can be extremely complex, especially with intangible assets like stock options. The first step is understanding how the law governs stock option ownership.

Generally, there are two legal systems that govern the division of stock options: community property and equitable distribution.

Community property. Under this legal system, all property acquired after the couple marries, by the work and efforts of both, is jointly owned and divided in half upon divorce. Accordingly, in the event of a divorce, neither spouse can sell, gift, or dispose of any of the property. Rather, a court must determine who owns which property, unless the parties enter into a legally sanctioned settlement.

As a general proposition, in community property states (Arizona, California, Idaho, Louisiana, Nevada, New Mexico, Texas, Washington, and Wisconsin), property is split equally between the spouses. Similarly, all debt is divided and apportioned equally between the divorcing parties. Any property acquired by gift or inheritance during a marriage is considered separate property, the sole property of the individual who received it. Separate property also includes the following:

➤ a pension fund that vested prior to marriage
➤ personal injury awards to one spouse
➤ a business created by a spouse prior to a marriage, although this may be deemed community property if the other spouse participates in the business

As with the division of real estate and other complex property, arguments could and often should be made that stock options are the holder's separate property. Timing is critical, as discussed below in further detail.

Equitable distribution. In this system, the property acquired during marriage is divided on an equitable basis. "Equity" is synonymous with the concept of fairness. Under this system the top income-earner in some cases may be entitled to two-thirds of the assets, while the other spouse receives the remaining assets. Courts generally look at a variety of factors, including the length of the marriage, the number of children, and the contribution of each spouse to the marriage, in dividing property under this system.

In most jurisdictions, stock options acquired during marriage are subject to equitable division. In all jurisdictions, courts consider when the stock options were acquired and the vesting schedule.

Timing Is Critical

WHILE THERE ARE MANY things to consider in dividing stock options upon divorce, timing is arguably the most important aspect. Stock options subject to community property division are those options received by the option holder between the date of marriage and the date of separation, which is generally the date when one spouse moves out with the intent to remain separate.

Stock options are also divisible as community property if the options were received prior to marriage and are exercisable before the parties separate.

As for options granted before marriage and exercisable after separation, these options may constitute partly community property and partly separate property. In these cases, the trial court must first determine the extent of the community- and separate-property interests in the options, a task called apportionment. Unfortunately, there are no hard-and-fast rules governing apportionment in cases where the options were granted before marriage but are exercisable after separation. The courts generally have broad discretion to adopt any equitable method of allocation.

In some cases, the number of options considered to be community property is the product of a fraction. The numerator of this fraction is the number of months between the start of employment and the date of separation, and the denominator is the number of months between the start of employment and the date when each option became exercisable. This fraction is then multiplied by the number of shares of stock that could be bought on the date that each option was first exercisable.

Formulas can be intimidating at first glance. However, it is important to determine exactly what the formula seeks to accomplish. In using formulas, courts and legal practitioners attempt to determine to what extent options were granted for past, present, and future services, and when those services occurred in regard to the duration of the marriage. Options earned by services performed during marriage are part of the marital estate and subject to divorce property settlement. The formula provided in the previous paragraph rewards past services, allocating to the community its share of benefits earned before separation but not realized until after separation. It was upheld by a California court as reflecting the extent of the marital effort in earning the contractual right to receive the benefits of the options.

Also in California, however, a different "time rule" formula was upheld by an appellate court. The numerator in that formula is the number of months from the date of grant of each block of options to the date of separation, and the denominator is the period from the time of each grant to its date of exercisability. This formula arguably produces a more equitable result, because that court found that the options were intended to compensate *future* performance.

Still other approaches can be used by the courts in place of the formulas introduced here. Another approach is used when the options are for the purchase of publicly traded stock. The idea is to calculate the value of the options during the marriage and award that value to the employee spouse, while the other spouse is awarded the equivalent value of other community property as of the date of separation. This effects a cash-out division, awarding the employee spouse the community-property portion of the options and awarding the other spouse community property of equivalent value. With this approach, the employee spouse bears the risk of such rewards, to the extent an increase in the value of the company stock results from that individual's job performance, the company's performance, or the economy.

The complexity of the varying approaches, formulas, and timing elements necessitate qualified legal counsel. To clarify, here is an example of one approach.

The Time Rule in Action

JOE AND ANN HAVE BEEN MARRIED for twenty years in California, a community-property state. A year and a half ago, Joe became chief executive officer of Widgets, Inc., and received options to buy 200,000 shares of Widgets common stock. The shares vest over two years, and the exercise price for buying each share is $20. Thus, after the first year Joe's option package vests 100,000 shares, and after the second year the remaining 100,000 shares vest, which means that Joe can, after two years, buy the entire package of 200,000 shares at $20 per share, no matter how high the purchase price for Widgets stock rises during that time. The Widgets stock now trades for $40.

Over the course of the second year, the marriage deteriorates, and the couple separates before the second 100,000 shares vest. Joe exercised and sold 50,000 shares while married, with a gain of $1 million. He decided not to buy the other 50,000 vested shares. How should the options be apportioned?

The $1 million gain is community property and should be split between the spouses, because it was "realized" during marriage as income. The more challenging issue relates to the 100,000 shares that have yet to vest and the 50,000 shares that have vested but have not been exercised. We need to apply the time rule. Here is the formula:

$$(x \div y) \text{ multiplied by } z = \text{Number of options considered to be community property}$$

x = Number of days between the date of separation and date of grant

y = Number of days between date of grant and date on which each portion of the stock received pursuant to the exercise of the option became fully vested and not subject to divestment

z = The gain or appreciation of the stock option on date of exercise

In Joe's case, he has worked for the company for eighteen months by the time he files for divorce. At $40 per share, the gain, or appreciation, on the vested 50,000 shares is $1 million. But as for the 100,000 shares that did not fully vest in the second year, when the marriage deteriorated and the couple divorced, we cannot know what the stock price will be when the options do vest. Thus, we need to use a valuation method, such as the Black-Scholes system, a complex calculation that is explained in greater detail in Chapter 2. Suppose this yields a valuation of $100,000.

For the 50,000 vested options, the formula looks this:

$$\frac{18 \text{ months} / 18 \text{ months}}{\$50,000} = \$50,000$$

Basically, since the marriage lasted as long as it took to vest the 50,000 shares, the complete gain is considered community property, so the spouses will split $50,000. Ann can either accept the option to buy 25,000 shares and not exercise them now, or she can exercise the 25,000 shares and either hold onto the stock or sell it.

Finally, let's apply the time rule to the unvested 100,000 shares:

$$\frac{18 \text{ months} / 24 \text{ months}}{\$100,000} = \$75,000 \text{ or } 75,000 \text{ shares}$$

The $75,000 is considered community property and is split between the spouses.

Options as Income

JUDGES HAVE WIDE DISCRETION in crafting divorce settlements and ordering property division. With options becoming a significant part of couples' financial situations, divorce courts have employed many different approaches, including characterizing options as income to the option holder.

Take the case of Richard and Deedee Kerr. After twenty years of marriage, the couple filed for divorce in a California court. Deedee was a homemaker and Richard worked at Qualcomm, with an annual salary of nearly $160,000. The couple had two children living at home.

Richard received stock options with substantial value. The court divided the options between the spouses and also awarded Deedee more than $3,300 per month in spousal and child support. Subsequently, Deedee requested a modification and asked the court to increase spousal support payments. The judge agreed with Deedee and raised the amount to $4,806 per month.

Why the change? The court characterized Richard's stock options as income. The rationale supporting the characterization was that the stock options provided a substantial amount of the family's income.

When the options were classified as income, they became part of the calculation for monthly spousal and child support. In fact, the judge went even further: He declared that Deedee would get 40 percent of all income from future option exercises until both children reached age eighteen. After that, she would get one-fourth of the income from option exercises. The parties subsequently settled the case.

Prenuptial Agreement

ONE WAY TO PROTECT THE TREATMENT and characterization of stock options is to prepare a prenuptial or postnuptial agreement. (A prenuptial is signed before a marriage and a postnuptial is signed during the marriage.) Over the past few years, prenuptial agreements have been used to allocate stock options, both vested and unvested. As this chapter demonstrates, the division of stock options is a difficult proposition. A prenuptial agreement can put to rest many difficult issues and even obviate protracted litigation.

Prenuptial and postnuptial agreements are enforceable to the extent they are properly prepared and executed. Agreements are generally enforceable unless they are constructed to encourage divorce, are prepared and signed without legal counsel for each party, or are inherently unfair. Since the law in this area is in a state of flux, qualified family law counsel is absolutely necessary.

Cohabitation

IT HAS BECOME MUCH MORE COMMON for people to forgo marriage and cohabitate, a situation with many legal ramifications. Some states recognize common-law marriages. Even though there is no marriage ceremony or license, under some state laws a couple is considered married if, for example, they have lived together for a certain amount of time or have indicated to people that they are, in fact, married.

Even in states that do not recognize common-law marriages, living together may have legal and financial consequences. For example, the couple may have an agreement that sets out division of property. Some courts find that there has been an implied contract, although this is difficult to prove. As with pre- and postnuptial agreements, consulting experienced legal counsel is not only a prerequisite but is often an excellent use of resources.

Summary

DIVIDING STOCK OPTIONS during a divorce is a difficult task with many steps. Obtaining qualified legal counsel is important, but equally crucial is developing an understanding of the questions and issues at stake. After determining whether the courts in your state employ a community-property or equitable-distribution system, you should next create a chronology documenting when the options were granted, when they vest, whether any have been exercised, and the dates of marriage and separation. The options must then be valued. Unless a pre- or postnuptial agreement divides the property, the following step is to think about how vested and unvested portions of the options shall be allocated and the goals that such allocation would promote. Finally, former spouses must either reach an agreement that is documented by qualified legal counsel or petition a court to divide all property.

Key Issues to Consider

➢ Each state has its own laws regarding divorce and stock options. The laws have undergone a great deal of change in the past few years as stock options have become a more important part of a family's income. It is critical to seek qualified counsel who understands the intricacies of your state's divorce laws.

➢ Courts have broad discretion regarding stock options. In fact, some courts consider stock options to be income and thus subject to the determination of child support and alimony.

➢ Because of the uncertainties of divorce laws and stock options, prenuptial and postnuptial agreements are becoming a method to allocate stock options, whether vested or unvested. This is an effective way to eliminate the uncertainties.

➤ Record keeping is very important. Make sure you have a chronology of your stock options: when they were granted, vested, and exercised.

C h a p t e r **15** *F i f t e e n*

Estate Planning

T HERE ARE MANY TERRIBLE STORIES of ineffective estate planning that depleted the transfer of wealth to heirs. One example is Joe Robbie, who died in January 1990. Because his estate tax bill was so huge, his heirs had to sell the Miami Dolphins and half of the Joe Robbie Stadium.

But don't think that estate planning is strictly for the wealthy. With your employee stock options, you may find that you *are* wealthy. Even if you're not, without a solid estate plan, estate taxes could severely deplete your wealth. Estate planning is not a fun topic to consider, but if you do not do it properly, your heirs will pay the price through an unnecessary reduction in their inheritance. This is especially the case with stock options, which are complex financial instruments that must be carefully factored into any estate plan.

Basics

WHEN YOU DIE, THE FIRST CONCERN of a financial nature is the status of your options. Most stock option agreements will set forth the terms. For both incentive stock options and nonqualified stock options, the agreement usually will indicate that your estate or beneficiary may exercise the vested portion of the options. Unfortunately, in most cases, your heirs will lose the unvested options—unless your contract contains an acceleration clause.

There may be a time limit on when the estate or beneficiary can exercise the options, usually within ninety days of your death. Since dealing with an estate is complex, however, some agreements may grant a year or more.

Remember: If you do not exercise an ISO option within ninety days of terminating employment, the ISO status is ended. Obviously, at death there is a termination of employment. If the exercise is not within ninety days, your heirs or estate risk losing the ISO status, unless the IRS makes an exception. Keep in mind that when ISOs are exercised in the event of a death, the transfer of the shares to the estate and heirs does not constitute a disqualifying disposition.

In regard to a beneficiary, you must look at your agreement to see if you can name one for your stock options. Now, the agreement may not mention beneficiaries, but you could ask your company to change the contract to allow for one.

If you can name a beneficiary, then request a beneficiary designation form from your company. Of course, naming a beneficiary is a highly complex matter with long-term financial ramifications, and it would be wise to seek the advice of a competent attorney.

Estate Taxes

AT THE TIME OF DEATH, unvested stock options have no tax consequences. This is the case if they are in-the-money. Of course, you owe taxes on vested options—even if they are unexercised. These options become part of your entire estate and are thus subject to estate taxes ranging from 37 percent to 55 percent.

This does not mean you will necessarily pay taxes, however. Each person has an exemption of $675,000 from federal estate taxes at death, although this amount will be steadily increased to $1 million by 2006. By using trusts, a married couple can use their combined exemptions to protect $1.3 million from federal estate taxes.

Employee stock options increasingly have substantial value and, as a result, trigger a sizable federal estate tax liability. For example, suppose you die, leaving the following assets: house ($500,000), stock ($300,000), car ($20,000), and unexercised vested options ($500,000). The estate will be required to determine the fair market value of the options at the time of your death. In most cases, this is calculated with the Black-Scholes model. Let's say that model values the vested options at $200,000. In that case, your entire estate is worth $1.02 million. After accounting for your exemption of $675,000, the remaining amount, $345,000, will be subject to federal estate taxes.

Taxes on Nonquals and ISOs

JACK WORKS AT XYZ and has unexercised nonquals with a fair market value of $200,000. These options have already vested. He suddenly dies, and his option agreement requires his beneficiaries to exercise the stock options. (If the beneficiaries are minors, their legal guardians would exercise the options on their behalf.)

Now suppose that Jack set up a trust that shielded his estate from any estate taxes and to which he transferred nonquals for his daughter, Jane, the beneficiary. The trustee must exercise the options on Jane's behalf and recognize the $200,000 gain as ordinary income. In other words, the options do not get a "stepped-up" basis.

There is an interesting wrinkle for determining the fair market value of the stock. In most cases, this is the average of the highest and lowest stock price on the day of the death. However, you may be able to use a six-month valuation if the total value of the estate proves to be lower at the six-month anniversary of the death.

Let's say that Jack had an estate worth $4 million and the nonquals were subject to estate taxes. In this case, Jane can receive a tax deduction for the estate taxes paid on the $200,000 of nonquals. So if the estate tax rate were 55 percent, the taxes would be $110,000. Jane can use this as a deduction on her income tax return.

If Jack had ISOs, the tax treatment would be very different. First of all, the beneficiary or estate would be required to exercise the options (usually within ninety days of his death). But the exercise will not result in any immediate tax consequences.

Also, there is the stepped-up basis. If it costs Jane $10,000 to exercise Jack's options, the cost basis would be $210,000, which is the $10,000 purchase price plus the $200,000 gain. Any subsequent sale of the stock would be considered a capital gain, with no need to meet the ISO holding requirement. If Jane holds the stock for at least one year, the gain will be long-term.

In fact, let's say that Jack exercised the options *before* he died. At his death, Jane receives the shares. If she sells them, she still gets the stepped-up basis and does not need to meet the ISO holding period.

Liquidity

THE FEDERAL GOVERNMENT requires estate taxes to be paid within nine months of death. This can be highly problematic for many people—especially those with illiquid assets like real estate, a family business, and even stock options.

For example, suppose you have an estate valued at $2 million, of which $1.8 million is in the form of stock options in your employer, XYZ. To pay the tax bill, the estate will need to sell off a huge portion of the stock, and this can substantially diminish the ultimate value of the estate that will eventually be transferred to your heirs. Also, what if XYZ is a private company? In that case, your estate probably will not be able to sell the stock. If it did so, it would be at a significant discount.

One way to provide liquidity for estate taxes is to use a life insurance trust. Example: You set up an irrevocable trust with an insurance policy that pays $500,000 at the time of your death. To pay for the policy, you pay $8,000 per year in premiums. The amount is tax-free, since it is under the $10,000 gift limit. When you die, the $500,000 is available estate-tax free for your heirs. This liquidity will allow them time to take appropriate actions with the options.

But there still can be some problems. There are annual letters that must be sent to the beneficiaries and other formalities that must be followed in order for the proceeds to pass tax free. Also, if you place an existing policy in the trust, then you must live for at least three years after the transfer. If not, the distribution at the time of your death is not tax-free. And remember that in order to get a life insurance policy, you need to be insurable, and you may not be if you have major health problems.

Gifts

ONE METHOD OF REDUCING potential estate taxes in general is to gift property before you die. Depending on the type of options you have and your employer's policies, you may be able to gift your stock options.

First, some background: Every year, you can gift assets with a maximum value of $10,000 per recipient tax-free. Let's say you and your spouse both work for XYZ Co. and have $500,000 each in fair market value of stock options (based on the Black-Scholes model). This means that together you can gift $20,000 of these options per recipient tax-free. You have three kids and a granddaughter, and you decide to give $20,000 to each, thus reducing the value of your estate by $80,000.

However, if your gift to someone exceeds $10,000 for the year, then you may be subject to gift tax, which you, not the recipient, pay. The gift tax is intended to prevent people from avoiding estate taxes by making lifetime gifts over the annual exclusion.

All gifts that exceed the $10,000 limit are first subtracted from your unified credit (this is your $675,000 exemption from estate taxes). Once this is used up, then you will need to make gift tax payments on any gifts exceeding $10,000.

Note that companies typically prevent employees from gifting stock options. Why? Well, a primary purpose of stock options is to motivate employees. By giving away stock options, the employee will not benefit from his or her work directly. Also, ISO options cannot be gifted because they must be held by employees. If you do transfer the options, the status will change from an ISO to a nonqual. Moreover, a company may limit the gift recipients to family members and trusts.

Once the gift is made, the recipient has discretion over when to exercise, but this may change. Say you give $10,000 in stock options to your son, John. However, after one year, you leave your job. Your employer then requires you to exercise the options.

Furthermore, when the options are exercised, it is you who pays the taxes, not John. That is, you will pay the ordinary income taxes on the difference between the exercise price and the fair market value of the shares underlying the stock option. John gets the shares tax-free, and the cost basis is equal to the stock price on the day of the exercise.

Limitations on Gifts of Options

SUPPOSE YOU WERE GRANTED 1 million options in XYZ, with an exercise price of 10¢. It is tempting to transfer these options as a gift, since their current value is probably zero. But suppose the stock increases to several dollars. Well, you would have effectively moved millions of dollars of value out of your estate.

This is why the IRS intervened on such maneuvers by issuing a Revenue Ruling in 1998. Basically, the valuation of a gift cannot be determined until it is classified as a completed gift. That is, the recipient of the gift must have control over the asset. If the gift is placed in a revocable living trust, or if an employee stock option is unvested, then the gift is not completed.

If you make a gift of stock options that is not complete, it is nearly impossible to predict the results. For instance, you gift the unvested options for 10,000 shares of your company to your daughter. In six months, the options vest. But during those six months, the stock price has soared. According to the Black-Scholes model for valuing stock options, the value of the gift at the time the shares vested is now $90,000. In this case, the gift may be subject to gift taxes because it exceeds $10,000.

Let's look at a completed gift. You have an option for 10,000 shares that have vested. You transfer the 10,000-share option to your son. At the time of the transfer, the option has a value of $10,000. Taxes are due only when the options are exercised.

After ten years, the stock of XYZ has soared to incredible heights. The shares are now worth $4 million. If you had not gifted these options and they had become part of your estate, the taxes could be as much as $2.2 million (55 percent times $4 million).

Trusts

TRUSTS ARE VERY POPULAR VEHICLES for shielding assets from estate taxes, and they can help you use your $675,000 exemption effectively. A credit bypass trust is a good example. Suppose you have been married for forty years, and when your spouse dies, his will specifies that his assets will be transferred to you. Ordinarily, you would not receive your spouse's $675,000 exemption. But if you set up a credit bypass trust beforehand, then $675,000 of your spouse's assets is automatically transferred to the trust when he dies. The trust can be structured to provide income to you, your children, or any other recipient.

If you have assets in excess of $1.25 million, consider a grantor retained annuity trust (GRAT). Under this arrangement, you place property in an irrevocable trust but have the right to receive a certain amount of income (the current IRS rate is 7.8 percent) over a fixed period of time. For example, suppose you exercise $500,000 in stock options and place the stock in a GRAT for ten years. You will be paid, say, $39,000 per year as a fixed annuity (the amount can be taken in either cash or stock). After ten years or your death, the remaining value of your trust goes to your heirs. Thus, if the value of the portfolio grows over this time, the amount can be substantial, while at the same time, you have been receiving income. The grantor retained unitrust, or GRUT, is a variation on the GRAT. With a GRUT, the annuity varies based on the value of the property within the trust.

Family Limited Partnerships

A FAMILY LIMITED PARTNERSHIP (FLP) is yet another way of shielding your assets. Let's say you have options in a public company. You exercise the options, which have a value of $1 million. You establish a family limited partnership and become the general partner, which means you have full decision-making control over the assets. This is the case even if you own only 1 percent of the partnership. You can then gift ownership interests in the partnership to your family members, or anyone else, for that matter.

But be advised that the limited partnership interest has a reduced value. First, the ownership interest is fairly illiquid (in other words, it is hard to sell a partnership interest). Second, the limited partner has no decision-making power. Because of this, the IRS allows you to take a discount on the value of this interest. In some cases, the discount can exceed 50 percent. Let's say you gift $20,000 of the partnership to your son. After applying the private market discount, the gift value would be $10,000 for tax purposes. In other words, with an FLP, you have the opportunity to gift your assets at a discount and thus ultimately realize large savings in estate taxes.

Charities

DEPENDING ON THE TERMS of your stock option agreement and stock option plan, you may be able to donate your stock options to charities. But again, the options must be completed gifts.

Many companies are reluctant to allow for charitable donations of stock options. As discussed above, such actions may lessen the incentive for the option holder to continue to work hard, since it is the charity that benefits, not the option holder.

If you are allowed to donate your options, you need to be aware of the following rules regarding charitable contributions:

➤ **Qualified recipients.** The charity must be a "qualified" organization. You can find a list of qualified organizations in IRS Publication 78.

➤ **Limits.** If the gift exceeds $250 per year for a charitable organization, the organization must submit a written statement to you. You attach a copy of the statement to your tax return.

➤ **Tax year.** You must make the contribution in the tax year you claim the deduction.

➤ **Valuation.** If the gift exceeds $5,000 and there is no reference of valuation (such as a stock price), then you need to get a qualified appraisal. This is the case with employee stock options of private companies.

But note that a lifetime gift of a nonqualified stock option to charity provides very little, if any, benefit to the option holder. Unlike a gift of appreciated stock, where you may deduct the fair market value of the stock from your adjusted gross income even though your basis is very low, there is no similar deduction for a gift of a stock option. You are not entitled to a deduction for the fair market value of the option at the time of transfer.

In addition, since the option holder has no basis in the option, there is no deduction at the time of the gift. Effectively, the assignment of the option is an assignment of income to the charity. When the charity exercises the option at some future time, the option holder has reportable income on the difference between the fair market value of the stock and the option exercise price. It is possible that, at the time of the exercise, the option holder will be entitled to an income tax deduction for the amount he was required to report because of the exercise by the charity. However, even if he is entitled to that deduction, it may be limited in the year of exercise by the percentage limitations on deductions for charitable contributions.

If that is the case, the option holder can carry the deduction forward, but he will not have a "wash" in the year that the option is exercised. Obviously, this is not a good result. Therefore, although it is possible to gift transferable stock options to charity, it is not the most effective way to satisfy your charitable intentions.

On the other hand, leaving a gift of transferable stock options to charity in your will may be a very effective method of satisfying your charitable intentions while maximizing the tax benefit for your family. Basically, if your options are transferable, you would specifically gift them, via your will, to a named charity or charities. Your estate would be entitled to a deduction for the fair market value of the options. And when the charities ultimately exercise the options, the income would be treated as income to the charity and not be taxable.

For example, let's say you have a $3 million estate with $500,000 of transferable options. You do not have a surviving spouse, but you do have two children, and you plan to make a bequest to charity of $250,000. If you simply gave the charity $250,000 of cash and the balance of your estate to your children, the remaining $2.75 million (including the fair market value of the stock options) will be subject to estate tax. When your children later exercise the options, they will pay income tax on the difference between the exercise price and the fair market value. There is an income deduction for estate taxes paid that will reduce the tax due, but there will still be an income tax due.

Therefore, from the $2.75 million, your children will receive an amount after the payment of estate tax and after the payment of income taxes from the options exercise. If, however, you satisfy your $250,000 bequest with options valued at $250,000, the income tax otherwise due will be payable by the charity. Since the charity is not paying income tax on the exercise, it receives the full value of the options. Compare this to the net amount your children receive because their inheritance is reduced by the estate tax on the full value and the income tax on the exercise.

Again, it is important to know the contractual or plan limitations, if any, on the ability to transfer your options before you incorporate a gift of options in your will. If you are certain that you are going to make stock option gifts in your will, you might want to have some discussions with your intended charity to make sure it is prepared to accept such a gift.

Heirs

YOU HAVE WORKED AT A START-UP for two years. During this time, the company has gone public, and your options are worth $50 million. You have a nineteen-year-old son from a prior marriage, and you did not remarry. When you die, your son will inherit the $50 million.

Obviously, a nineteen-year-old probably will not be mature enough to deal with such a huge sum of money. In fact, there is a good chance that he will spend the money wildly.

To avoid the problem, you can create a trust with a spendthrift clause as part of your estate plan. This places limitations on the heirs. For example, you might require that your son go to college in order to receive some of his estate money. Or you might distribute, say, $50,000 per year to him. You have a great deal of flexibility.

Executors

AN EXECUTOR WILL ADMINISTER your estate when you die. Therefore, when selecting someone for that very important role, make certain the person has a strong financial and tax background— and, of course, understands the intricacies of stock options. Too often, people select friends to serve as executors—people who often do not have any kind of financial, legal, or tax expertise. This can be a big mistake, and your heirs are likely to pay the price. As an alternative, consider having an attorney or a bank serve as executor.

Conclusion

MAKING A MISTAKE WITH your estate planning can obviously be very costly—especially when dealing with the complexities of stock options, which can be quite volatile. In order to make good decisions, take a thorough look at different scenarios. Some computer-based simulations can do this, but unfortunately, they are expensive. Attorneys and CPAs who specialize in employee stock options should have the necessary tools to craft an effective strategy.

Once you have set up your estate plan, you have done the vast majority of the work, but not all of it. In the fast-paced world of changing careers, you need to periodically review your estate plan to ensure that it still accurately reflects your financial, family, and job circumstances. A good rule of thumb is to review the plan every six months. When you have major changes in your life—such as your job, divorce, marriage, death, and so on—you should also revisit the plan. Estate planning is a dynamic process.

Key Issues to Consider

➤ When you die, there is usually a time limit for when the estate can exercise vested options (usually ninety days). If the options are not exercised by then, they will be worthless.

➤ Highly valued options can result in a large estate-tax bill. One strategy is to set up an insurance policy to pay for the tax.

➤ Each person can gift $10,000 to any person without paying gift taxes. This technique is often used to shift money out of your estate to lower your estate taxes. Although you can gift stock options, the gift must be completed (the options need to be vested).

➤ Another way to shift money out of your estate is to gift your options to a charity.

➤ When naming an executor of your estate, make sure he or she has an understanding of the financial, legal, and tax requirements of your stock options.

Afterword

W E ARE WITNESSING the proliferation of stock options as a form of compensation. Options for four billion shares were granted between 1994 and 1998 by corporations in the Nasdaq 100 Stock Index, according to an August 15, 1999 article in the *New York Times*. The popularity of the stock option is easy to understand. The option presents a win-win proposition to all the players: presumably, the harder the option holder works, the more the company will benefit and the greater the appreciation in the value of the company stock.

Until the recent downturn in the stock market, stock option grants generated considerable publicity. Options made some high-tech executives and employees millionaires almost overnight, or so it seemed at the time. You now know, after reading this helpful guide on stock options, that there's more to it than that.

Options have little or no value if the company's stock is diluted or, worse yet, if the company fails, as we saw in the Introduction and Chapter 2 of this book. In some cases, the tax liability associated with an exercise of options may significantly diminish the expected gain, and, as we saw in Chapters 3 and 4, the overall tax picture may not be clear without the assistance of experienced tax counsel or a certified public accountant. In other cases, as discussed in Chapter 5, without legal counsel, certain key individuals may be required to return all profits from stock option exercises to the company for failing to comply with short-swing rules that are embodied in securities laws. In Chapter 14 we learned that stock options are subject to complicated rules of division upon separation and divorce.

In light of the complexity and uncertainty surrounding stock options, one thing is for sure: this book accomplishes its objective of discussing stock option issues in user-friendly terms. It is not designed to provide legal advice, and it should not be construed as such. The readers should keep in mind that a book, no matter how masterfully written, is not a substitute for qualified and individualized legal counsel and tax advice. Professional expertise is an absolute necessity in dealing with the complex issues that stock options can raise.

STEPHEN T. FREEMAN, J.D., AND GARY J. VYNEMAN, J.D., LL.M.
Stradling Yocca Carlson & Rauth
Attorneys at law
Newport Beach, California

Appendices

Appendix A:
Web Site Resources

Fairmark Press

www.fairmark.com

At this site you will find a section called "Compensation in Stock and Options." The comprehensive guide covers such topics as vesting, exercising, incentive stock options, nonqualified stock options, and so on. The focus is primarily on the tax consequences of stock options.

The author of the site, Kaye A. Thomas, is a tax attorney at Ungaretti & Harris, a leading law firm based in Chicago. He earned his law degree from Harvard Law School.

The MDE Group

www.mdegroup.com

The MDE Group is a consulting firm that specializes in advising clients on employee stock options. The firm is compensated on a fee-only basis (it does not earn commissions on the products it recommends) and consists of a team of attorneys, CPAs, MBAs, and CFPs. The firm was founded in 1987.

MDE has developed a sophisticated software technology called the Option Optimizer. The software helps to manage the risks and returns of employee stock options, as well as estate planning, retirement planning, and cash flow budgeting. However, the software is mainly for option-planning professionals.

MyInternetOptions.com

www.myinternetoptions.com

This firm provides valuation services for your stock options. This is helpful for a variety of situations, including the following:

➢ Estate settlements
➢ Comparing two or more career opportunities
➢ Calculating your net worth
➢ Evaluating the differences between options with and without repricing

The fees for the service range from $10 to $149. The site also contains a glossary, FAQs, and articles.

myStockOptions.com
www.mystockoptions.com

MyStockOptions.com is a comprehensive online resource center for executives, employees, and consultants with stock compensation. The founders and advisory board members of myStockOptions.com are respected leaders in financial planning, tax, and legal topics related to equity compensation. Features include:

MyRecords. You can track your options and monitor important items like expiration and vesting dates.

Calculators. These tools help you model different scenarios, such as "Should I exercise now or later?" There is also an "I Need the Money" calculator, in which you specify the amount you need and the calculator finds the optimal strategy.

FAQs. This section includes more than 400 FAQs and their answers, with stock option and equity compensation topics that range from basic to sophisticated.

Global Resource. This section has details on the stock option laws of twenty-five countries.

Ask the Experts. You can ask the myStockOptions.com experts all the tricky questions you can think of.

Discussion Groups. You can chat with others who have employee stock options.

Articles. The site includes links to more than 100 articles from online and print publications. New articles are added monthly.

National Association of Stock Plan Professionals (NASPP)
www.naspp.com

The NASPP is an industry organization for employee stock professionals. Of the organization's 6,000 members, most are stock-plan designers or administrators.

National Center for Employee Ownership (NCEO)
www.nceo.org

NCEO is a nonprofit organization that provides research about employee ownership of companies. The organization covers not only employee stock options but also employee stock ownership plans (ESOPs) and employee stock purchase plans.

Membership is $70 per year, but note that the organization's benefits are geared to stock-option professionals, not option holders. However, the site does have valuable content, such as articles, columns, and links, as well as the NCEO Library, which offers a comprehensive discussion of employee stock options.

OptionWealth
www.optionwealth.com

OptionWealth is a comprehensive site that includes articles, frequently asked questions (FAQs), news stories, and glossaries for stock options. The site also has valuable online option-planning tools, including the following:

Tracker. This software enables you to track your options in real time. It can even handle stock bought on the market, restricted stock grants, and shares from employee stock purchase plans. Include in the portfolio any margin debt you might have. Of course, you can perform Black-Scholes calculations with your holdings, too. Tracker also has alerts for vesting dates, expirations, days remaining for favorable capital gains treatment, and price targets.

Strategy Room. This sophisticated tool lets you look at various scenarios for exercising and selling option holdings. The software accounts for cash flows, taxes, margin borrowing, and 83(b) elections.

Forecaster. Part of creating stock-option strategies is predicting the future stock price. Of course, this is no easy feat. However, the Forecaster allows you to perform statistical calculations based on historical data to estimate future stock prices.

Optimizer. This tool takes the information from Tracker, Strategy Room, and Forecaster to create a comprehensive financial plan for your stock options. To do this, the Optimizer considers all of your financial assets, as well as your tolerance for risk. The results of the Optimizer are based on professional best practices from the accounting, legal, estate planning, and financial planning professions.

Salary.com
www.salary.com

This site deals with salary and compensation issues in general and also has a great section on stock options. This section offers an options overview, terms and definitions, and sample stock option plans. It also covers topics such as tracking stocks, current grant practices in high-tech companies, vesting and exercising, tax implications, and negotiations. The site also provides some excellent charts and tables on stock option practices, vesting schedules, and percentage ranges for executives in the high-tech industry.

Stock-Options.com
www.stock-options.com

This site is designed for employees, officers, and directors of public corporations, and it offers guidance in calculating, inventorying, and analyzing employee stock options. It features a calculator (non-secure) with which to keep track of your options, a comprehensive set of links, and discussion forums.

Appendix B:
Stock Option Glossary

MANY OF THESE TERMS have additional meanings in the world of bonds, commodities, and publicly traded options such as puts and calls. The definitions given here focus only on those meanings that relate most directly to incentive stock options.

83(b) Election. Within thirty days before the grant, an option holder is allowed to exercise the options. Any further taxes from the appreciation of the stock will be considered a capital gain. In order to make an 83(b) election, a letter must be sent to the IRS.

401(k). A retirement plan provided by a company. Through tax-deferred payroll deductions, an employee will set aside a certain amount of money periodically. The money can be invested in mutual funds or, in some cases, the employer's stock.

423 plan. See Employee stock purchase plan.

Accredited investor. A person who is considered by the Securities and Exchange Commission to be sophisticated enough to buy high-risk investments, such as private placements. Accredited investors must meet the following requirement: they must have a net worth of $1 million, exclusive of their homes, or they must have earned at least $250,000 per year for the past two years.

ADR. See American Depositary Receipt.

Affiliate. A "control" person in a company, such as an executive, major shareholder, or director.

After-hours trading. Systems that allow individual investors to place trades for several hours after the Nasdaq market closes.

Alternative minimum tax (AMT). A separate tax system, complementary to the regular federal income tax system. The purpose of AMT is to make sure that wealthy taxpayers do not take advantage of too many deductions. When incentive stock options (ISOs) are exercised, the shareholder might owe AMT. Determining that is a complex process. You must look at your overall tax situation to see if the

AMT applies. Such things as mortgage interest deductions, capital gains, and medical expenses can have major effects on AMT.

American Depositary Receipt (ADR). A share of common stock of a foreign company that is traded on an American stock exchange.

American Stock Exchange (AMEX). Now part of the Nasdaq (National Association of Securities Dealers Automated Quotation System), AMEX lists mainly medium-sized companies.

Amount realized. The amount of proceeds you obtain when you sell a stock after deducting all fees, such as commissions.

Analyst. A person, usually employed by a financial firm, who follows a certain basket of stocks or an industry sector and issues investment opinions on them, such as buy or sell recommendations.

Annual meeting. A company's officers and directors have a one-day meeting with shareholders. At the meeting, shareholders vote on such matters as mergers, stock option plans, and elections of directors. If a shareholder is unable to attend, he or she can have a third party vote his shares through a document known as a proxy.

Annual report. A public company must publicly release this document within ninety days of the end of its fiscal year. It must also be filed with the Securities and Exchange Commission. The annual report is a comprehensive document on a company's finances, management, legal proceedings, and executive compensation.

Ask. In a stock trade, the price at which a seller offers to sell a stock.

Assets. The property of a company. The property can be tangible (cash or buildings) or intangible (patents).

Auditor. A third-party firm, usually an accounting firm, that determines the accuracy of a company's financial statements. This is a requirement of the Securities and Exchange Commission for any company that wants to trade on a major stock exchange, such as Nasdaq or the New York Stock Exchange.

Authorized shares. The maximum number of shares that a company has the power to issue to the public. This is determined by a vote of the shareholders.

Balance sheet. A financial statement showing a company's assets, liabilities, and net worth at a certain time.

Basis. *See* Cost basis.

Bear market. An extended period of flat or declining stock prices.

Beneficial owner. A person or entity that solely owns or shares the ownership of stock. Commonly, a beneficial owner is a person who has the same rights as the owner—such as voting or selling—except that the shares are held in another name. The most common example of this is when a venture capital (VC) firm invests in a company. The VC firm has a fund composed of an assortment of investors. The VC firm determines what companies to invest in and becomes the beneficial owner of the shares.

Beneficiary. Someone who is the recipient of an inheritance or of assets from a trust, annuity, or insurance policy.

Best-efforts offering. A sale of stock to the public in which the underwriter does not guarantee to the issuing company that the desired level of money will be raised.

Bid. In a stock trade, the price the prospective buyer is willing to pay.

Big Board. See New York Stock Exchange.

Blackout periods. Certain times of the year when company employees—in most cases, the insiders—are not allowed to sell their stock or exercise their options. The main purpose of this is to avoid the possibility of insider trading during certain events, such as the announcement of quarterly earnings or an upcoming merger. The Securities and Exchange Commission mandates blackout periods.

Black-Scholes option pricing model. A complex mathematical equation for the valuation of employee stock options. The model takes into account a variety of factors, such as volatility of the stock and dividends.

Block. A large amount of stock traded with one order—say, 10,000 shares, or shares worth more than $200,000.

Blue chip. The stock of a large, well-regarded company, such as Disney, IBM, or GE.

Blue-sky laws. State laws regulating the sale of securities. In order for a company to do an IPO, it must comply with these blue-sky laws for any state in which the shares are offered.

Board of directors. A group of people approved by the shareholders to help with major strategic issues, such as mergers and acquisitions, dividends, joint ventures, stock option plans, and major investments. The board typically meets every month.

Boiler room. Industry jargon for an open office from which small brokerage firms trade stocks in small companies. These brokers typically use high-pressure tactics.

Bull market. An extended period in which stock prices are rising.

Call option. The right to buy 100 shares of a stock at a stated price for a certain period of time (usually three months). There is no obligation to exercise the call option. This is similar to an employee option; however, call options are traded by investors on an open market.

Capital gain. The amount realized when you sell your stock at a profit. If the sale occurs within one year, it is considered a short-term capital gain, and the ordinary income tax rate applies. If the stock is sold after more than one year, then it is a long-term capital gain, and the tax rate is 20 percent.

Capitalization or capital structure. The mix of instruments used to fund a company, such as preferred stock, common stock, and long-term bonds.

Capital loss. The amount you give up when you sell your stock for a loss. You can deduct up to $3,000 in capital losses on your tax return.

Cash account. Another name for a basic brokerage account, in which an investor deposits money and can buy and sell stock.

Cash basis. *See* Cost basis.

Cash exercise. Exercising your stock options by using cash as the form of payment.

Cash flow statement. The inflows and outflows of cash generated from the operations, investments, and financing of a company (usually tabulated on a quarterly basis). All public companies must file their cash flow statements with the Securities and Exchange Commission.

Cashless exercise. A practice facilitated by brokerages in which you do not have to present cash to pay for the exercise of your options. Rather, a brokerage firm will lend you the money to buy the stock and immediately resell it. The net proceeds (after deducting a commission) will be sent to you. Not all companies allow cashless exercise of their stock options.

Certificate. A document that is evidence of stock ownership in a company. The certificate will have such information as the number of shares owned, the name of the company, the address of the shareholder, and an identification code.

Certified equity professional (CEP). A person who has completed a three-level self-study certification program for equity compensation. The program is administered by Santa Clara University, in California.

Certified public accountant (CPA). A certified public accountant is a licensed professional who provides services such as tax preparation. Some CPAs specialize in providing tax planning for employee stock options.

Churning. A stockbroker generates unnecessary trading activity in order to create more commissions.

Classified stock. Some companies have different types of common stock. For example, Class A shares may have more voting rights than Class B stock.

Cliff vesting. All of the shares of an option grant vest on the same day.

Closed corporation. See Privately held company.

Commission. The fee paid to a broker for buying and selling stock.

Common stock. Shares issued to investors that represent part ownership in a company. With common stock, an investor typically has such rights as voting for mergers and directors and may be eligible to receive dividends.

Compensation committee. Most public companies have a special committee that determines the broad matters of employee compensation: pensions, executive pay, and stock options. The members of the committee are usually company directors.

Confirmation. A statement sent to a client documenting the purchase or sale of a stock.

Cost basis. The amount it cost a shareholder originally to buy stock in a company. The cost basis is compared to the amount received when the stock is sold in order to determine the size of any capital gain or capital loss.

CPA. See Certified public accountant.

Current assets. Assets likely to be converted into cash within one year. Examples include accounts receivable and inventory.

Current liabilities. Debts owed by a corporation that are payable within one year, such as accounts payable and wages.

Day order. A stock trade that will be canceled at the end of the trading day if it is not triggered by conditions specified by the investor placing the order.

Delisting. Removal of a company from a stock exchange because it has fallen below the exchange's minimum requirements, such as number of shareholders or sufficient assets.

Direct placement. See Private placement.

Direct public offering (DPO). A company sells shares to the public without using the services of an underwriter. Typically, DPOs are very small and illiquid.

Discount broker. A firm that transacts stock trades at a steep discount compared to full-service brokers. Many companies use full-service brokers to handle stock option transactions.

Disposition. The transfer of stock to another person or entity. This can be through sale, inheritance, or gift.

Disqualifying disposition. Occurs when a person (1) sells stock that was acquired as a result of exercising incentive stock options before two years have passed since the options were granted; or (2) sells the stock within one year of the exercise. When a disqualifying disposition has occurred, you are unable to get favorable tax treatment. *See also* Holding period.

Diversification. Spreading investment funds among a variety of different types of assets. In theory, this should help reduce the overall risk of a portfolio.

Dividend. A cash payment to shareholders, usually made quarterly. The dividends are paid from the profits that the company generates. Some companies do not pay any dividends to shareholders.

Dow Jones Industrial Average (DJIA). A weighted average that tracks the performance of thirty top companies, such as Disney, Microsoft, and Intel.

Dual listing. When a stock is listed on more than one stock exchange. For example, a stock might be listed on the New York Stock Exchange as well as on foreign markets or regional U.S. exchanges.

Earnings per share (EPS). A measure of how "cheap" or "expensive" a company's shares are relative to its capacity to generate revenue and profits. EPS is computed by dividing the net income of a company by the number of shares outstanding.

EDGAR (Electronic Data Gathering, Analysis, and Retrieval System). A huge database maintained by the Securities and Exchange Commission. Public companies must submit their SEC-required filings to this database. The Web address is www.edgar-online.com.

Employee stock ownership plan (ESOP). A written document that sets forth the terms of an option plan, such as the vesting period, type of options, and number of shares available to be granted to employees.

Employee stock purchase plan (ESPP). This allows employees to buy stock in the company by using payroll deductions. In most cases, the employee can buy the stock at a 15 percent discount to the market value. An ESPP is also known as a 423 plan, named after the section in the IRS Code.

Evergreen provision. A clause within an option plan that allows for a certain increase in the number of shares available for the plan that can be issued by the company. The purpose of the evergreen provision is to give a company flexibility in increasing the number of shares without obtaining a vote from the shareholders.

Exercise. The purchase of stock that was granted to you in a stock option grant.

Exercise price. The price at which you buy the stock when you exercise your stock option. The exercise price is usually equal to the fair market value of the company's stock at the time of the option grant.

Expiration date. The date on which your stock options expire. Usually, an expiration date is expressed in the stock option plan. The maximum time allowed is ten years, or five years if you own more than 10 percent of the company.

Fair market value (FMV). The amount a company's stock is deemed to be worth on a given date. If a company is private, then the FMV is usually determined by an outside appraiser or based on values of comparable businesses. If the company is public, then the value is the price at which the company is then trading on the stock exchange.

Fiduciary. A person or entity that holds assets for another, known as the beneficiary. The fiduciary is legally required to act in the best interests of the beneficiary.

Financial statements. The reports of companies that include the balance sheet (assets, liabilities, and net worth), income statement (profits or losses), and cash flow statements (inflows and outflows of cash). Sometimes referred to as "financials."

Firm-commitment offering. An IPO in which the underwriter guarantees that it will buy shares in the company at a specified price.

Fiscal year (FY). Any twelve-month period used for the annual accounting of a company. It could coincide with the calendar year, although some companies start on different dates, such as November 1 or June 1.

Float. The number of shares that are held by the general public. If the float is small—say, under 5 million shares—then the stock may be subject to much volatility. Furthermore, it may be difficult for option holders to sell their holdings. *See also* Market capitalization *and* Outstanding.

Form 3. Within ten days of a person or company becoming an insider, he or she must file a Form 3 with the SEC indicating the insider's holdings (if any) of the company's stock.

Form 4. If an insider makes any changes in holdings of the company's stock, then he or she must file a Form 4. The document must be filed ten days after the end of the month in which the change occurred.

Form 5. A company must file this report with the Securities and Exchange Commission to show the annual changes in ownership of company insiders. The document is filed within forty-five days after the end of the company's fiscal year.

Form 8-K. A company files this with the Securities and Exchange Commission to disclose the terms of major transactions, such as mergers and acquisitions.

Form 10-K. This is similar to a company's annual report. However, whereas the annual report is a glossy document (typically containing many graphs and pictures), form 10-K is a pure text report filed with the SEC.

Form 10-Q. See Quarterly report.

Form 1099. Companies are required to send this statement to all their paid contractors. The statement indicates the amount of income the contractor earned during the previous tax year. The company also sends a copy of the statement to the Internal Revenue Service. If the person is an employee rather than a contractor, then he or she receives a W-2 form. *See* Form W-2.

Form S-8. A statement filed with the SEC to register stock for an employee stock option plan. Form S-8 must be filed before people can sell stock in the plan.

Form W-2. If you are an employee of a company, you will receive

W-2 statements indicating how much you made in salary or wages and how much was withheld in taxes. Some types of income generated from stock options will be listed on form W-2. *See also* Form 1099.

Formula plan. A stock option plan in which the recipients are granted a fixed number of shares.

Full-service broker. A firm that charges relatively higher commissions than discount brokers but provides more services. Many companies use full-service brokers to handle stock option transactions for their employees.

Gain. See Capital gain.

Generally accepted accounting principles (GAAP). The standards set by the Financial Accounting Standards Board that American companies use when preparing their financial statements.

Going public. See Initial public offering.

Good-till-canceled order. A stock buy or sell order that is canceled when the trade is executed or the investor decides to cancel the order, whichever comes first.

Grace period. In an employee stock option agreement, a company may specify a maximum period within which an employee can exercise stock options. The grace period may be extended for such things as termination, death, and disability.

Grant. Occurs when a company issues you stock options.

Holding period (for incentive stock options). Incentive stock options receive favorable tax treatment if stock is sold at least two years after the options are granted or one year after they are exercised. If the holding period is not met, the sale is considered a "disqualifying disposition."

Illiquid. An investment that is difficult to convert to cash without a substantial discount in its selling price. Many private companies, for example, are illiquid, because it is difficult to find buyers for their stock.

Immaculate option exercise. This is a cashless exercise in which the price of the shares being bought is paid by withholding a certain number of shares upon the exercise. That is, part of the shares of the exercise are being used to pay for the transaction.

Immature incentive stock option shares. Shares of stock acquired by exercising incentive stock options that have not met the holding requirement. The holding requirement is two years after the options are granted or one year after they are exercised.

Incentive stock option (ISO). A type of compensatory stock option, available only to employees of a company, that has certain tax benefits. When you exercise an ISO, you may be subject to the alternative minimum tax.

Income statement. The financial statement that indicates the profits or losses of a company. An income statement covers a certain period of time, usually three months.

Initial public offering (IPO). A company sells shares to the public for the first time. The company will thereafter be traded on a stock exchange, such as the New York Stock Exchange or Nasdaq.

Insider. An officer or director of a public company, or a company or person who owns 10 percent or more of any single class of a public company's stock.

Insider trading. Occurs when a person trades stock based on material information that is not known to the general public. In such cases, civil fines and even criminal sanctions can be imposed.

Institution. A major investor, such as a pension plan, mutual fund, or college endowment.

Intangible asset. An asset with no physical qualities, such as patents, trademarks, brand names, and franchises.

In-the-money. In compensatory stock options, the condition that exists any time the fair market value of the stock is higher than the exercise price of the option.

Issuer (of an option). The company that grants stock options to an employee.

Leave of absence. An arrangement with your employer allowing you to leave your company on a temporary basis, usually without pay. These arrangements may have unfavorable tax consequences or, even worse, the employer may revoke incentive stock options.

Legend. A statement on a stock certificate indicating that it is restricted. Restricted securities are those that have been issued in a private transaction and may not be sold unless certain requirements are met (such as a holding period).

Limit order. An order to buy a stock at a specified price or lower, or to sell a stock at a specified price or higher.

Listed security. A company that is trading on a stock exchange.

Lockup provision. A provision in the agreement between a company doing an IPO and its underwriter. The lockup provision restricts specific people—usually most of the employees and investors—from selling stock of a company within a certain period of time after an initial public offering. The typical time frame is six months.

Maintenance fee. The fee—usually $50 to $100 annually—that is levied by a broker on the holder of a brokerage account. Not all brokers levy such a fee.

Margin. A loan against an investor's stock holdings. The money can be used to buy more stock or other things, such as personal assets.

Market capitalization (market cap). The total market value of a company based on its current stock price. For example, if a stock is trading at $10 per share and there are 10 million shares outstanding, then the market capitalization is $100 million ($10 times 10 million shares).

Market order. An order to buy or sell stock at the best possible price immediately.

Mature shares. Shares of incentive stock options that have met the holding requirement. The holding requirement is stock that is sold two years after the options are granted or one year after they are exercised.

Money market fund. An open-end mutual fund that invests in highly liquid instruments, such as short-term government securities, corporate debt, and certificates of deposit. The interest is passed on to the shareholders, more commonly known as holders of money market accounts.

Mutual fund. An investment that pools many investors' money and then buys stocks of various companies. Some funds also invest in bonds and commodities.

National Association of Securities Dealers (NASD). An organization of the Nasdaq stock exchange that helps enforce the securities laws.

National Association of Securities Dealers Automated Quotation System (Nasdaq). A stock exchange made up of a myriad of computers and advanced telecommunications networks. The companies listed on this exchange tend to be smaller than those on the New York Stock Exchange.

Net income. The amount of profit a company generates.

New York Stock Exchange (NYSE). The oldest and largest stock exchange in the world. The requirements for listing on the NYSE are stricter than those for Nasdaq.

Nonqualified stock option. A compensating stock option that does not have favorable tax advantages. When you exercise the stock option, you must recognize ordinary income on the difference between the fair market value of the shares and the exercise price. In some cases, you may even be taxed when you *receive* a nonqualified stock option.

Nontransferability restriction. A clause in a stock option agreement that prohibits the transfer of stock to another person or entity. There are exceptions; one is for option holders involved in a divorce in a community property state.

Odd lot. A stock transaction involving fewer than 100 shares. *See also* Block *and* Round lot.

Officer. A top executive of a company. An officer is usually considered an insider and thus is subject to certain SEC rules.

Option. There are two types of options: investment options and compensatory stock options. Both are contracts that allow a person to buy a certain number of shares of a company at a certain price (known as the exercise price). With an investment option, a buyer and a seller take opposite sides of the trade and thus speculate on the potential value of the option. The option expires within a maximum of three months. Compensatory stock options, on the other hand, are granted to employees or contractors of a company and are not publicly traded. Usually a certain period of time (known as the vesting period) must elapse before a person is able to exercise the option.

Option agreement. A contract between you and your employer that sets forth the terms of the option grant. Terms include exercise price, number of shares, and so on.

Optionee or option holder. The person who receives stock options.

Option plan. A legal document that states a company's general option policies, such as types of options (incentive stock options or nonqualified stock options) and vesting.

Ordinary income. Income that is not given preferential tax treatment, such as wages, commissions, and certain types of stock option income.

Out-of-the-money. Describes the status of an option whenever the fair market value of the stock is below the exercise price of the option.

Options that have no current cash value because they are out of the money are also known as "underwater options."

Outstanding. The number of shares of a company on the open market that investors can trade. *See* Float *and* Market capitalization.

Paper profit or loss. The change in portfolio value when a person's stock holdings increase or decrease in value but the person has not sold anything.

Par value. An arbitrary amount assigned to each share of common stock for bookkeeping purposes. Par value has no economic significance.

Penny stock. A company whose shares trade at less than $1 per share. Typically, such shares do not perform well over the long term.

Performance-based stock options. Stock options that are granted only if the company or the option holder achieves certain goals, such as increasing sales by a stated amount.

Phantom stock award. A setup in which an employee's cash compensation is based on the performance of the company's stock. Such incentive arrangements do not include any right to buy shares. *See* Stock appreciation right.

Pink sheets. Jargon for the market in very small stocks, usually penny stocks. This market tends to be illiquid and has problems with market manipulation and hype. The term "pink sheets" harks back to the days when red paper was used to print stock quotes for this marketplace. Now pink-sheet stocks are traded on electronic exchanges.

Point. The basic unit of measurement of a stock's price. A point is equivalent to $1.

Preferred stock. Shares in a company that have preferential features for the holder. For example, holders of preferred stock get dividends before common shareholders do. Also, holders of preferred stock will get assets in a liquidation before holders of common stock will.

Privately held company. A company that is not traded on a public stock exchange. Determining the value of the company's shares usually requires an outside appraiser or a valuation based on comparable companies in the industry.

Private placement. A sale of securities to accredited investors and not to the general public.

Profit-and loss-statement. *See* Income statement.

Prospectus. The legal document that must be provided to investors when raising money from the public, such as for a mutual fund or stock in a company. The prospectus, which is required by the Securities and Exchange Commission, has comprehensive information on the company: financial statements, biographies of the management, industry background, and product or service descriptions.

Proxy statement. A document required by the Securities and Exchange Commission that is sent to shareholders to give them the opportunity to vote on company issues, such as executive pay, mergers and acquisitions, and even the employee stock option plan (a proposal to expand the number of shares in the plan, for instance).

Public offering. *See* Initial public offering.

Qualifying disposition. A stock transaction that meets certain IRS requirements for preferential tax treatment. The term applies only to incentive stock options (ISOs), which may be taxed as capital gains. *See also* Disqualifying disposition.

Quarterly report. A document discussing the quarterly results of a public company, such as finances and recent activities (mergers, stock splits, or the creation of a tracking stock). A quarterly report must be filed within forty-five days after the end of a company's first three fiscal quarters each year.

Quotation. The current price at which the latest trade was made in a stock.

Red herring. Another name for a preliminary prospectus used by a company's underwriter in anticipation of an initial public offering. The name comes from the SEC warning to investors printed in red on the front cover. *See* Prospectus.

Regional stock exchange. A U.S. stock exchange located outside of New York City. Examples include the exchanges in San Francisco, Boston, and Philadelphia.

Registered representative. *See* Stockbroker.

Registration. The process through which a company files documents with the SEC to allow for its stock to be traded on a stock exchange.

Regular-way delivery. The customary delivery and payment for stock transactions, in which the buyer must pay cash and the broker must deliver stock certificates within three days of the transaction.

Reload provision. A feature in an option plan or option agreement wherein a new option grant may be exchanged for an old one. The new exercise price is usually the current market price.

Repricing. Occurs when a company reduces the exercise price on existing stock option agreements. When the stock price has fallen significantly and the company does not want employees to leave because their options have no value, repricing is a choice the company may consider.

Restricted securities. Shares that are issued in a private placement and are not registered with the Securities and Exchange Commission (SEC). They cannot be sold unless certain requirement are met (such as being held for a specified period or being registered with the SEC). These securities are also called Rule 144 Stock.

Reverse split. A company reduces the number of shares outstanding. For example, shareholders may receive one share of new stock for every two shares of old stock, at twice the current price of the old stock. The purpose of this is to boost the stock price, especially for shares that have fallen below $1.

Round lot. A stock trade that is in increments of 100 shares.

Rule 10b-5. The Securities and Exchange Commission rule against insider trading. *See* Insider trading.

Rule 144. An exemption under the federal securities laws that allows persons with restricted stock to sell their positions.

Rule 144 stock. See Restricted securities.

S-1. See Prospectus.

Same-day sale. See Cashless exercise.

Section 16(a). A provision under the Securities Exchange Act of 1934 that requires insiders of a corporation to file their holdings and changes in beneficial ownership.

Section 16(b). A provision under the Securities Exchange Act of 1934 for the so-called short-swing rule. *See* Short-swing profits recovery rule.

Section 83(b) election. A statement filed by an option holder with the IRS within thirty days of receiving a stock-options grant. By filing the 83(b) election, the option holder is choosing to recognize stock options as ordinary income. The income is calculated by finding the difference between the fair market value of the stock and the exercise price. All future gains will be subject to capital gains tax.

Securities Act of 1933. A federal law that regulates the issuing of securities to the public. The act requires companies—unless there is an exemption—to disclose material information to investors. Material information includes such matters as financial results, mergers and acquisitions, dividend announcements, and stock splits.

Securities and Exchange Commission (SEC). The governmental agency that enforces the securities laws, such as the Securities Act of 1933 and the Securities Exchange Act of 1934.

Securities Exchange Act of 1934. This act regulates the disclosure required of companies that are already public. For example, public companies are required to make quarterly and annual reports as well as filings for important matters such as mergers and acquisitions.

Selling short. An investor borrows stock and then sells it immediately on the open market. In the future, the investor will be required to buy the stock back in order to repay the lender of the stock. The investor hopes that the stock price will then be lower. In other words, selling short is a method of making money when a stock falls in value.

Share. See Common stock.

Shareholder. A person who owns common stock, restricted stock, or preferred stock. A person who owns options is not considered a shareholder.

Short-swing profits recovery rule. Under this provision of the Securities Exchange Act of 1934, insiders are not allowed to make short-term profits in trades in the company stock. Short-term is defined as six months. If the rule is violated, the insider must return the profits to the company.

Short-term gain. Selling a stock within one year. The trade is taxed at the same rate as ordinary income.

Spin-off. A division of a company that is sold to the general public in the form of an initial public offering.

Split. See Stock split.

Spread. In stock trading, the difference between the bid and ask prices of a stock. Typically, in small stocks, the spreads are relatively higher. In stock-option parlance, the spread means the difference between the exercise price and the fair market value of the stock.

Statutory option. See Incentive stock option.

Stock. See Common stock.

Stock appreciation right (SAR). An agreement with an employee whose compensation is based on the growth of the company's stock over a certain period of time. The amount is paid in cash, not in stock. SARs are not stock options. *See also* Phantom stock award.

Stockbroker. A person or firm licensed by the National Association of Securities Dealers that executes stock trades on your behalf. Many companies have standing agreements with a stockbroker to handle stock option transactions for their employees.

Stock exchange. A marketplace in which stocks are bought and sold. Examples include the New York Stock Exchange and Nasdaq. While the New York Stock exchange has a physical trading floor where buyers and sellers trade stock, the Nasdaq is a virtual exchange, in which trades are made via computers.

Stockholder. See Shareholder.

Stock option. See Option.

Stock split. A company increases the number of shares outstanding. Typically, this is done as a 2-for-1 stock split; that is, for every share of stock existing, one more is issued. The price of a share is reduced by one-half to reflect the 100 percent increase in the number of shares outstanding. Most stock option plans have adjustments for stock splits.

Stock-swap exercise or stock-for-stock swap. Exercising stock options by paying for the stock with shares you already own, not cash.

Street. Also known as Wall Street. *See* New York Stock Exchange.

Street name. Stock certificates that are held for safekeeping by a brokerage firm. This typically makes it easier to administer such transactions as buying and selling the shares.

Strike price. See Exercise price.

Subsidiary. A majority-owned or wholly owned division of a bigger company. Sometimes employees of a big company will get stock in the subsidiary for which they work, not in the bigger company.

Swap. See Stock-swap exercise.

Syndicate. A group of investment banks that helps sell stock to the public in an initial public offering (IPO).

T+3. Shorthand for the usual term of settlement of stock trades. Within three days of a T+3 trade, the seller receives cash and the buyer receives shares from the transaction.

Tax basis. See Cost basis.

Tax deferral. Taxes on a transaction are postponed and the realized gains of an investment will be taxed later. This is often done with retirement vehicles, such as individual retirement accounts (IRAs) and 401(k)s.

Tax withholding. See Withholding.

Term. The amount of time an employee has to exercise stock options. The maximum allowed term is ten years.

Termination. The ending of an employment relationship. Such an event can have many consequences for the employee's stock options. For example, if the termination is for cause, the employer may cancel all of the stock options. ISOs must be exercised no later than three months after termination.

Transferable stock option. A stock option that can be transferred to another person or company. This can be done as a gift, as a sale, or through death (such as in a will). Incentive stock options are generally not transferable, but nonqualified stock options are more flexible.

Transfer agent. A firm that administers the transfer of the stock certificates when stock is transacted. The transfer agent has a database of all current stockholders to make sure that all transactions are completed with respect to dividends, stock splits, and financial reports.

Treasury shares. Shares that were once outstanding but have been repurchased by the company.

Underwater. See Out-of-the-money.

Underwriter. A firm that prepares a company to do an initial public offering. Basically, an underwriter buys a certain amount of stock from the company and then resells the shares to the public at a higher price, thus generating a profit for the underwriter.

Unvested shares. Stock options that an employee cannot yet exercise.

Venture capital firm. An investment firm that invests in privately held businesses. These firms typically look for high rates of return, which often are found in high-tech industries.

Vesting (of compensatory stock options). The process by which options mature. For example, typically a person must wait a certain period of time after an option is granted, such as one year, before he or she is permitted to exercise the option.

Vesting (of stock bought via compensatory stock options). Even after someone has exercised stock options, he or she may still be prohibited from selling the stock on the open market. There may be resale restrictions with time limits. When these restrictions expire (or the stock vests), the person can freely sell the shares.

Wall Street. *See* New York Stock Exchange.

Withholding. An employer will deduct a certain amount of taxes from an employee's compensation. Withholding is required when a person exercises nonqualified stock options.

Index

About Bloomberg

Bloomberg L.P., founded in 1981, is a global information services, news, and media company. Headquartered in New York, the company has nine sales offices, two data centers, and 79 news bureaus worldwide.

Bloomberg, serving customers in 100 countries around the world, holds a unique position within the financial services industry by providing an unparalleled range of features in a single package known as the BLOOMBERG PROFESSIONAL™ service. By addressing the demand for investment performance and efficiency through an exceptional combination of information, analytic, electronic trading, and Straight Through Processing tools, Bloomberg has built a worldwide customer base of corporations, issuers, financial intermediaries, and institutional investors.

BLOOMBERG NEWS℠, founded in 1990, provides stories and columns on business, general news, politics, and sports to leading newspapers and magazines throughout the world. BLOOMBERG TELEVISION®, a 24-hour business and financial news network, is produced and distributed globally in seven different languages. BLOOMBERG RADIO™ is an international radio network anchored by flagship station BLOOMBERG® WBBR 1130 in New York.

In addition to the BLOOMBERG PRESS® line of books, Bloomberg publishes *BLOOMBERG® MARKETS*, *BLOOMBERG PERSONAL FINANCE™*, and *BLOOMBERG® WEALTH MANAGER*. To learn more about Bloomberg, call a sales representative at:

Frankfurt:	49-69-92041-200	São Paulo:	5511-3048-4530
Hong Kong:	85-2-2977-6600	Singapore:	65-212-1200
London:	44-20-7330-7500	Sydney:	61-2-9777-8601
New York:	1-212-318-2200	Tokyo:	81-3-3201-8950
San Francisco:	1-415-912-2980		

FOR IN-DEPTH MARKET INFORMATION and news, visit **BLOOMBERG.COM®**, which draws from the news and power of the BLOOMBERG PROFESSIONAL™ service and Bloomberg's host of media products to provide high-quality news and information in multiple languages on stocks, bonds, currencies, and commodities, at **www.bloomberg.com**.

About the Author

Tom Taulli is a specialist in the initial public offering field and has written about the stock market for a variety of publications, including *Barron's, eCompany Now, Research* magazine, *Individual Investor,* and *Registered Representative.* He also writes columns on IPOs for such online publications as CBS MarketWatch, internet.com, and Forbes.com. Currently the Internet stock analyst for internet.com, he is a regular on CNBC and CNN, and is the author of *Investing in IPOs Version 2.0.*